LOVE IS
SOMETHING
YOU DO

A HARPER JUBILEE BOOK

Harper Jubilee Books

1 WILLIAM BARCLAY: The Life of Jesus
   for Everyman

2 ERNEST GORDON: Through the Valley of the Kwai

3 HELMUT THIELICKE: The Waiting Father

4 PAUL TOURNIER: The Person Reborn

5 A.W. TOZER: The Knowledge of the Holy

6 WALTER TROBISCH: I Loved a Girl

7 WALTER TROBISCH: I Married You

8 ELTON TRUEBLOOD: The Humor of Christ

9 ETHEL WATERS: To Me It's Wonderful

10 ELEANOR SEARLE WHITNEY: Invitation to Joy

11 SHERWOOD ELIOT WIRT: Not Me, God

12 JOHN R. BISAGNO: Love Is Something You Do

13 INGRID TROBISCH: The Joy of Being a Woman

14 RICHARD WURMBRAND: Victorious Faith

LOVE IS SOMETHING YOU DO

John R. Bisagno

A HARPER JUBILEE BOOK

HARPER & ROW, PUBLISHERS
New York, Evanston, San Francisco, London

A HARPER JUBILEE BOOK FIRST EDITION

Library of Congress Cataloging in Publication Data

Bisagno, John R
  Love is something you do.
  (Harper jubilee books ; 12)
  1. Marriage. I. Title.
BV835.B55 1975   248'.4   75–9314
ISBN 0–06–060792–0

Contents

Preface   vii

1. Marital Mathematics (+ and − Theory)   1

2. The Difference Makes the Difference   11

3. Love Is Something You Do   19

4. On Being in Love and Loving   23

5. You Can Fall in Love Again   29

6. When You Have to Forgive   40

7. The Bed Undefiled   47

8. Sex—the Unselfish Gift   54

9. The Forbidden Fruit   61

10. The Perfect Bond   68

11. Ride Those Wild Horses   74

12. Is Divorce Ever Right?   78

13. Love in the Bedroom   84

14. Love All Around   93

To my favorite young couple, my darling daughter, Ginger, and her handsome preacher-husband, Curt.

Preface

For the past twenty-one years I have been in the people-helping business. The churches I have pastored have been characterized by one thing: the presence of hundreds of sharp, attractive, married young couples in their twenties and thirties. Because they are people, they have problems. Because they are sensible people, they want answers to those problems.

Within a few short days of my first full-time pastorate, I found myself caught up in a whirl of marital counseling. After a few years it became obvious that everyone has basically the same problems with the same cause and effect. The needs of most married couples are both classic and textbook cases. When one approaches the solving of these cases with the proper Biblical, psychological, and practical perspective, the answers are as easy as they are obvious.

Most common of all divorce charges is "incompatibility." But in that very incompatibility lies the potential for fulfillment in marriage. After all, we marry not because we are alike, but because we are different. What could be worse than being married to someone like yourself! In any marriage, two people bring together a powerful set of dynamic personality characteristics comprised of assets and liabilities. In the ideal marriage, God brings together two personalities whose opposites perfectly complement each other. Even in the not-so-perfect marriage a miraculous blending of the two into perfect oneness can be a reality, a heaven on earth. Yes, it is within the marital grasp of us all, for marriage is a divine institution.

Jesus said, "Seek ye first the Kingdom of God, and His righteousness; and all these things shall be added unto you." Nowhere in life is He more interested in the affairs of His children than in seeing them achieve the potential of which they dreamed the day they stood at the marriage altar. Strange, isn't it, that the same sun that melts the ice also hardens the clay. Just so, the exchanging of those vows can begin a lot of difficulty and divorce, or a wonderful oneness. Regardless of which road you now journey, we shall through these pages see with new insight what God wanted for you and your mate when He gave you to each other.

JOHN R. BISAGNO

First Baptist Church
Houston, Texas

1

Marital Mathematics
(+ and − Theory)

While two persons play a similar role in marriage, they are, in fact, two different types of personality. The masculine and feminine roles ideally are clearly definable in the personality of husband and wife. God did not create Eve from Adam's feet to be trampled beneath him, nor from his head to be lord over him. He made her from his side, the nearest place to his heart, to be his equal.

Yet, as in all incidents of equality, there must be leadership. A successful football team moves as one organic unit. Mutual interest, compatibility, harmony, unity, and oneness all characterize such a team, but there must be a quarterback, a signal caller, a captain, a leader. Such is the case in God's plan for marriage. The husband is God's appointed head of the home, the leader in the marriage. Scripture teaches that he is the covering of the wife. In his masculine role he is provider, defender, captain, and hero to his wife and family. He is the aggressor, the quarterback. The basis of that leadership, however, is not automatic; it is not demanded. It is deserved and won and earned.

1

When the Apostle Paul requires that the wife honor the husband as the head of the home, he adds that the husband is to love his wife in precisely the same manner that Christ loved his bride, the church. And how was that? Christ loved the church unselfishly—to the point of death. That is always, to use the Greek New Testament word, *agape* (unselfish) love. Even *eros* (romantic love) and *phileo* (brotherly love) have an air of selfishness about them. We love that we might be loved in return. We love and give because there is something we hope to receive. But God's love— *agape* love—is always devoid of any selfish motive whatsoever. Regardless of the object, regardless of the circumstance, regardless of condition, God loves simply because He is God and it is His nature to love. Through the years, I have found that when a woman is loved like that, she is only too happy to honor her husband as the head of the home and to turn her body, soul, and life over to him who has expressed selfless love toward her.

Psychologists tell us that there must be an input from two kinds of personalities into the emotional development of children. A father must play the masculine role; the mother, the feminine. It is imperative to the well-being of the home, to the emotional stability of the children, and to the marital union of husband and wife. I like to think of these two roles as a plus and a minus. This is not to indicate that femininity, the minus, is zero, zilch, nothing; I am, rather, simply using an identification like the plus and minus of two posts in a battery. It is absolutely imperative, however, to understand that regardless of the role she is trying to

2

play, every woman wants to be a "minus." She wants to assume the feminine role. She wants to be cared for, loved, petted, provided for, made to feel she is controlled and overpowered by her hero, made to feel like a woman. For only when she feels like a woman can she express her true femininity.

The nature of the woman is the minus nature. Her ego is feminine. If it is masculine, she is outside her innate role as a person. What is a woman's ego but her femininity, and a man's, but his masculinity? If a man, for example, begins to feel his ego slipping, if he begins to have serious doubts about himself and bad feelings about his own self-worth and self-image, he may turn to affair after affair, trying to bolster his own self-worth by supporting his masculinity, for the two are inseparable. A man or a woman with a sagging ego may turn to some type of ego defense-mechanism: projection, sublimation, compensation, withdrawal, denial, but always something to reinforce the feminine or masculine role that he or she must play for psychological fulfillment.

When asked what is the greatest commandment, Jesus said, "Thou shalt love the Lord thy God with all they heart, . . . and thy neighbor as thyself." Notice that He said "as thyself." In these brief words He summed up the three most important truths for emotional, spiritual, social, and physical well-being:

(1) It is wonderful to love God.
(2) It is commanded to love others.
(3) It is normal to love yourself.

All psychologists agree that the epitome of mental health and emotional well-being is a good, healthy self-image, good ego structure. In the words of Jesus it is that you love yourself. The self that a woman loves is a feminine self, a minus self, and the self that a man loves is a masculine self, a plus self. The man that a woman loves is the "plus" man who makes her feel more of a "minus" woman by virtue of her comparative relationship to him. The woman that a man loves is the feminine, "minus" woman, who makes him feel more of a "plus" man by their relationship.

At this point we must be careful not to misinterpret the characteristics which comprise true masculinity and femininity. To be feminine does not necessarily mean to be soft, quiet, and dainty. To be masculine does not necessarily mean to have broad shoulders and bulging biceps. A small, frail man may be very much of a plus if he is strong in character. A large woman may be very feminine if she is tender in spirit and if she is loved selflessly, wooed and won by a man who makes her feel like a queen.

I cannot overemphasize the importance of the plus-minus roles in the man-woman relationship. A woman may be happy to play the feminine role in relationship to one particular man but not to another. For if a man is not a plus to her, he cannot make her feel like a minus by comparison. Likewise, a man who himself is a very strong plus may make her feel like a minus in relationship to him. In short, it may take certain masculine characteristics to make a woman feel like a woman in his presence.

We do not exist well apart. When God makes two people for each other, He sees that there are characteristics in one that the other needs. There are psychological fulfillments in one to offset needs in the other. There are pluses for minuses and minuses to fulfill pluses in each of them, and not just any man can fulfill the total emotional, psychological, and spiritual needs of just any woman. It is what they are when they are together, what they are as one, that makes them complete. The charge in the battery does not occur until the plus and minus cables meet and their forces interact with each other. Then the electric shock occurs and the power flows. Unfortunately, not every man is a plus or every woman a minus, but the man who is a whale of a plus can make a plus woman feel like a minus by comparison. And the right woman can make a plus out of a minus man.

Obviously, there are four potential combinations of personality relationships:

1. PLUS MAN—MINUS WOMAN

Ideal relationship for both.

2. MINUS MAN—PLUS WOMAN

Domineering wife. She assumes the masculine role. She becomes the family leader, the initiator, the discipliner of the children, the bill-payer, the dominant force in the home. Result: husband often withdraws. His own feelings of insignificance intensify, and his wife assumes a mother image to him as well as to his children. This type of relationship, though far less than ideal, can be tolerable for two reasons:

A. The plus woman has never met a man who was plus enough to make her feel like a minus by comparison, and she simply does not know that anything better exists. Her true femininity lies dormant, and though she may occasionally feel inadequate, she is content to let well enough alone. She compensates for the frustration caused by her inability to feel like a woman by assuming the masculine role and is more the plus image to her children and a mother image to her husband. Her greatest problem is that she is not aware of the cause of her frustration and that it may have a devastating effect on her children before whose eyes the proper role has been twisted.

B. Further, she will likely compensate in social relationships and be disliked by her peers who see her as a "horsy" woman. Ultimately she may find her only true companionship with other horsy women. To her, feminine women are weak. Femininity in herself will become increasingly less desirable as the masculine role perpetrates itself, and all because she is not married to a man who is enough of a plus to bring out the femininity which lies forever unawakened inside of her.

3. MINUS MAN—MINUS WOMAN

In some ways this may be the best of the second-best relationships. The two minuses do not have much to offer, nor do they require much. They never do much. Their lives are slow, and they tend to become very cautious. Being weak, they become very dependent upon each other and, finding little support there, tend to become progressively content to be what they are—not much of anything! How many double minuses do you know? I know many of them, and they are not necessarily unhappy or particularly happy. They are just alive, just there. The tragedy is that a plus man could bring this minus woman to life, but she is hardly aware that such life exists. The man's weakness is intensified by the fact that having little to contribute himself, he has nothing to bring out in the woman, which would in turn bring out something in himself. The two perpetrate their nothingness upon each other, and they live quietly, though not too happily, ever after.

4. PLUS MAN—PLUS WOMAN

This, to me, is the most interesting of relationships because it is fraught with exciting potential. One of the popular beauty ads suggests that if you want him to be more of a man, try being more of a woman. I could not state too strongly that apart from the miraculous power of spiritual conversion to Christ and the resultant divine operation of His Spirit, the human personality is hard to change. What we are, we are! But by His power we *can* change.

A woman executive, an independent type, is exciting. If her husband dies, she won't fall apart.

She will pick up the pieces and go on. She can handle the insurance and pay the bills. She is so constituted that she cannot live exclusively in a world of baby powder and spanking bottoms. She is what she is, and her very plus quality intensifies the obvious—that she is a woman with deep feeling, full of life, virility, and potential. When the feminine characteristics which are present in her being are awakened, she is a fantastic person. She has class, charm, vivaciousness. But *it takes a whale of a plus man to make this plus woman a minus by comparison!* When her femininity is awakened, when she is brought to life by just such a plus man, she is a wife and lover and mother and person, vibrantly alive, tinglingly exciting, and excited about life.

Again, it takes a whale of a plus man to make a minus out of a plus woman. The beauty of the gospel of Jesus and the transforming effect of His power upon human personality is that a man *can* be made a sufficient plus, so vibrantly alive to life, so totally fulfilled as the wild horses of human nature come to harness, that he can make his wife respond as a minus by comparison. He can awaken her femininity by the rebirth of his own masculinity.

What is masculinity in the eyes of a woman? I don't mean the cheap movie heroines or the glamorized, oversexed playgirl. I mean real women, women whose true femininity is expressed, not just in curves, but in class, not just in the bedroom, but in the living room, women of quality and character. To a real woman, masculinity is not just a Saturday-afternoon football hero. It is a man of character. He is a man like the most gentle, soft-spoken, and yet rugged man among men who ever lived—Jesus Christ himself. For when Jesus Christ lives inside of a man, He begins to reproduce Himself in that man, and that man becomes like his Lord.

Jesus did not say, "Blessed are the weak." He said, "Blessed are the meek." A meek man has all the wild horses of human nature. He is explosive and dynamic. He may be quiet, but he is not quaint. He may be solid, but he is not soft. He is consistently cool, faithful, steadfast, gentle, dependable, kind, courteous, thoughtful, loving. He is the man with the wild horses under control. He is a man's man, and this kind of a man is a woman's man too. Jesus Christ has been in the business of making this kind of plus man for a long, long time.

A word to you who are about to be married. Young woman, make dead sure you marry a plus. Don't think that just because he has long hair, sparkling eyes, a cute mustache, or is a "cool daddy super swinger" that he is a man. Does he tell the truth? Is he dependable? Does he get a job and keep it? Does he always gripe about those for whom he works? Does he fault-find and bicker, does he pick on you and criticize you? Does he seem to be projecting his own misery and making you miserable? Back off from him and look at him long and hard, for unless he's got that kind of real coolness, Sam super swinger will wear awfully thin through the years.

To you who are married, take hope. Any man can be made new. A real man is a Christian man.

What woman would not idolize Billy Graham? What woman would not adore Jesus Christ? These men are men in every sense of the word. In the musical *Jesus Christ, Superstar,* a woman who met Him said, "I don't know how to love Him." There was never a man quite like this man. Any woman who can respect and idolize a man who was a man like Jesus Christ will be very much a woman. That is the kind of man that for centuries Jesus has been making out of men who will let Him.

2

The Difference Makes
the Difference

As no two snowflakes are alike, so there are no two human beings alike. How many parts comprise a human personality? A hundred, a thousand, a million? No one knows. Each of those individual personality characteristics in relationship to all the rest of them make for infinitesimal billions of possibilities.

Into every marriage relationship two people bring a powerful set of personality characteristics. Let's look at them again in terms of pluses and minuses. A person has tens of thousands of pluses, strengths, assets, powers, areas where he can offer, where he can support. But he also has thousands of needs, weaknesses, failures, liabilities. *In the ideal marriage, a person is joined with a perfect opposite, a partner who exactly fulfills his or her need, who has strength for the spouse's every weakness, an asset for every liability, a plus for every minus.*

One of the great fallacies of our modern society is the computer dating service. This is a supercilious system which is supposed to bring together people who are ideally suited for each other simply because they have the same pluses. They are both patient. They both like opera. They both enjoy Mexican food, and neither one graduated from high school, so they are supposed to be ideally suited. Tommyrot! What could be more boring than being married to someone exactly like yourself? For you are, in effect, only loving the self which you project into your partner and which you see in him. You are only loving yourself in return.

That is precisely the plight of the homosexual and precisely the reason that God gave them up in the Book of Romans. God gave them up because they loved themselves so much that the only thing they could love was a projection of their own selves in the life of another, and they were, in fact, loving themselves in return. Consequently, they ultimately lose the capacity to love anything or anyone but themselves. They cannot love others normally; so they become homosexual. Neither can they love God normally. Giving up *on* God, they are given up *of* God.

The approach that suggests compatibility in marriage as a mere projection of loving someone who is exactly like yourself, whose pluses are your pluses, whose minuses are your minuses, is fatal to a marriage. It is fatal to life because life is to be found in dying. Receiving is the result of giving; fulfillment is found in selflessness. The giving of self to the satisfaction, enrichment, and fulfillment of others is in reality the fulfillment of one's own self. Where is that area of marriage in which the blending, the compatibility, the giving occurs? Is it where the plus meets other pluses? Of course not. It is where a plus encounters a minus. It is in the area of opposites, for only here can both people yield and give.

The difference makes the difference. Unless there can be a give and take, a mutual sharing, unless two people have something to offer each other while receiving something that they need in return, what is the use of being married? It is not in the areas of similarities, it is in the areas of difference, the contrasts, the unlikeness, that the benefits of marriage accrue. There is someone in this world who is the perfect counterpart of your every need, who is strong everywhere you are weak, and who has an asset everywhere you have a liability. Ideally that someone is the partner to whom you are married if it has been God's wedding, God's marriage.

Then why do people divorce? Because our shallow-brained society has bred into our thinking the totally false concept that if there are differences, areas of dissimilarity, contrast, then husband and wife are not compatible. The only thing to do is split the sheet. How absurd! This is what marriage is all about. Two people can find the differences in their marriage partner to be a perfect balance to their own needs. In this area giving and strengthening and growing occur; here two people become one. The problem areas are where the fun is. Look at it sexually. If a man has no sexual needs, he does not need a sexual partner. But he does have them, and he marries. He also has a thousand other needs that can only be met by that ideal partner; and only God knows who he or she is and only God knows how to put that marriage

13

together. You can ask Him to help. You can seek His assistance. He is, after all, the creator of human personality, the Great Psychologist.

Let's look again at our "ideal" marriage partners created by the modern computer dating service.

They both like Mexican food, but Mexican food is rich, spicy, fattening, and hard to digest. Too much of it can give you heartburn and ulcers. If the husband is inclined to live on Mexican food, he will have trouble. It is a potential problem for him. His wife is similar so she has nothing to contribute. Being alike they only compound each other's problem and get heartburn!

Now imagine she were different. Suppose he lives on Mexican food, but she is a health fadist and lives on goat's milk and organic vegetables. Because they are so totally different, they have supposedly become incompatible. She will not give, and he will not give. The answer? Get a divorce. Right? Wrong! How long can you live on goats milk? The girl needs a little spice in her life. She needs to have a few tacos with him. What about him? He is going to kill himself. He'd better eat some of her vegetables, and regularly. The difference makes the difference; they contribute to each other.

Oh, yes, they both like opera and that's all! What a boring life to enjoy nothing but opera. Every life needs a little Dixieland. You don't want to get too stuffy, now do you? Their life-style becomes insipid and boring. They are stuffy and self-sufficient, and they tend to get proud, those supersophisticates! They need to loosen up a little and learn to laugh. If she were a Dixieland nut, she could brighten him up occasionally. But if she were only a Dixieland buff, she would probably be giddy and silly. She needs a little refinement, polishing, a little opera. If they were different, they could both give a little, contribute a little to each other, for they each have so very much to offer of what the other needs.

And they are very patient, both of them. Patiently dull, boringly so, and being that kind of personality can lead to such extremities that one can hardly act at all. Decisions frighten him. To be forced to a commitment, to make up his mind, to decide, can be a traumatic experience. He misses all the good deals and good jobs because he cannot act. He is afraid of wrong decisions, afraid to run the risk of failure; so he never enjoys the risk of success. He doesn't get that job, he doesn't make that deal. They didn't have any money this month, and they can't pay the bills. She hates him; they see a marriage counselor; he suggests they get a divorce. They are supposedly incompatible. But are they really incompatible? Not at all. The real problem is in their similarities. They are both so overly patient they have compounded each other's problem to near fatality.

Had they been opposite, had she been the kind who acted too slowly and he the impetuous type, they would have been good for each other. If they had yielded, there was so much to contribute in the area of their differences. When the plus met the minus, the plus could have learned caution. He could have learned to act more slowly, to temper his impetuosity. Her minus could have been

15

greatly aided by his plus. He could have brought her out of her reserve. He could have taught her to act in faith, to go ahead and accept the calculated risk of failure in order to win the fruits of success.

They are an "ideally suited" couple. Both are high-school dropouts. But had he been a Ph.D., he could have lovingly encouraged her to finish her education, to gain confidence in herself, to go to night school, to take some college hours. He could have contributed greatly to her own ego and self-image. But, they are supposedly incompatible, and they divorce. They miss the beautiful area of the difference, the realm in which both can contribute to each other.

Jesus, in reference to marriage, said, "For this cause shall a man leave father and mother, and shall cleave to his wife; and they twain shall be one flesh." Sexually one flesh, yes, obviously; but He meant far more than that. In the earthly tabernacle of this fleshly body reside emotion, knowledge, will, character, mind, heart, soul, and psyche. Inadequate personalities, incomplete people, people who need other people, are indeed the luckiest people in the world. When two opposite personalities begin to mesh, when the many thousand personality characteristics of two personalities begin to merge in marriage, a miracle should occur. But without divine help, they begin to grind and clatter and clash like sand poured in the carburetor and usually end in frustration at best and divorce at worst.

When, however, the meshing, merging parts of those same two people begin to blend by the well-oiled presence of God in their lives, heaven can occur. Psychologically, spiritually, and emotionally two people may become so much one, so complete, so fulfilled, that only as they are fulfilled by the other can they know true contentment. A day, a week apart can be emotional agony, not simply sexually, but in that they are not complete, not whole as personalities because that one who has literally become "the rest of them" is away. Think back through your childhood to those old family reunions when you used to see that great aunt and uncle, that great-grandmother and grandfather, who had been married fifty or sixty years. Remember how through the years they began to think alike, talk alike, act alike, and, yes, even look alike! The two had become one. The divine operation was being enacted. The needs of two individuals were being completed, and all the minuses were finding fulfillment in the pluses of their opposite.

At some time in your life many of you will seriously consider divorce. You will look at the areas of your life where you are alike and receive pleasure. You will look at the areas of conflict and difficulty and find unhappiness. Look again! There is hope for your marriage! Where you are already strong, where you are already fulfilled, where characteristics of your life are already assets, you have no need. There you can benefit nothing from your partner, but you can contribute TO him.

Look at the differences. Look at the problems and rejoice! If God has brought your marriage together, you have a plus for her every minus and

17

a minus for her every plus just as she has for you. Take those areas of difficulty to the Lord in prayer. Hold them up to Him, let the Heavenly Psychologist teach you where you may both contribute, both give. He will reveal to you the perfect, corresponding plus to your every minus, where you can receive and where you can give. The blending, meshing parts of the two will make one perfect and beautiful whole. The difference makes the difference!

3

Love Is Something You Do

The Bible speaks of three kinds of love: *agape,*
God's love; *phileo,* brotherly love; *eros,* romantic
love. When the Gospel writers used the words *eros*
and *phileo,* they always used them in the context
of human relationships. Only a man can love a
woman romantically and sexually. Only a man
can love his fellow-man with *phileo* love, for both
are human love, and consequently both contain a
degree of selfishness. There is the beautiful response of the romance, both anticipated and
desired. But when we come to *agape* love, heavenly love, we find it distinct and unique. It is
marked by total absence of any selfish motive. It
is love because God is love. It loves because the
object of love is there, and that is enough. The
object does not have to be beautiful or desirable,
nor does it have to deserve God's love or even want
God's love. Yet, it is loved because agape love,
loves. Period! That is the kind of love which He
gives to us and which He desires that we should
give to others.

As His people, He commands us to love. "If you
love me, keep my commandments." "Greater love

19

hath no man than this, that a man lay down his life for his friends." "By this shall all men know that ye are my disciples, that ye love one another." In no case is love equated with emotion. It is always action. Love, far more than what one feels, is what one does. We, like our heavenly Father, are to love, not because the object of our love is lovable, deserving, or even wishes to be loved, but simply because as God's children, we love.

This most beautiful word in the English language is perhaps the most misunderstood and the most abused. We say in the same sentence, "I love the Lord, and I just love pizza." "I love my children, and I love my job." What are we saying when we speak so of love? Are we not saying that love is a gratification of my own desires? The Apostle said, "Love seeketh not its own." Love is selfless, love gives, love suffers, love sacrifices, love does not want the best for itself; it wants the best for the other.

Often a boy will say to a girl, "If you love me, you would." He is actually saying, "I want to use you. You are the object of something I need and want. It would satisfy me for you to cooperate, and if you really love me, then you want me to be satisfied and happy, and so you will give me your body." But he doesn't know what he is saying. Let the girl say to him, "If you love me, you won't because you will not take something from me that I do not wish to give. My peace of mind, my self-respect, my hope for tomorrow, my self-worth, my purity, my virginity." For while *eros* and *phileo* love have an ingredient of selfishness and are, therefore, not the kind of love that God is capable of

20

LOVE IS SOMETHING YOU DO

having but can only be expressed on a human level, *agape* love, divine love, is desired by God in our every earthly relationship. This, He says, is how we are to love, how we are to act. Most of all it is how we are to act in the holiest of relationships, the beautiful expression of romantic love that is the marriage bond.

We are commanded to love, expected to love, most of all our own spouse. But how can we love someone whom we honestly may not love? The answer to this can be seen only in terms of a new understanding of the meaning of the word *love.* Careful reexamination of the words *love, loved,* or *to love* in the New Testament reveals a very surprising truth. Nowhere is love defined in terms of the emotional. Love is always equated not with what one feels, but with what one does. *Love is something you do.* "If you love me, you will obey my commandments." He says, "If you love your wife, you will treat her selflessly, sacrificially as Christ did His bride, the church, and died for her." This is not to say that emotional love, romantic love, affectionate *eros* love, may not be in our relationships, for most certainly they should be. One would hardly want to marry without it, nor would one want to live without it. But life is not built on emotion. It may produce actions just as actions may produce emotions, but love is something you do.

We find ourselves often in the dilemma of the young man who sent his beloved a note declaring, "I love you with all my heart. I would cross the burning desert to look into your eyes. I would climb the highest mountain to be by your side. I would forge the swollen river and swim the mighty ocean for a glimpse of your lovely face. *P.S.* I'll be over tonight if it doesn't rain."

The young man thinks he is in love, but real love cares and acts whether the emotion is there or not. Real love goes far deeper than movie-land romances and teen-age crushes. It gives, it bleeds, it hurts, it sacrifices, it cares, it dies. To die for a friend, to die for one's country, to die for one's wife, said our Lord Himself, is the greatest love a man can show to his fellow-man. Be it man or wife, friend or relative, country or institution, love is giving . . . love is doing. To love one's husband or wife is to act selflessly in relationships of life toward them for their own strengthening, up-building, and edification. In this kind of giving, love begins to flow back into the heart of the giver which can make him a man among men, a king among kings. Women interpret very much what a man says in light of what he does. Always the verbal expression of love should be present in a home. Always the romantic and emotional should be in a marriage, but it is the action of kindness and selflessness which keeps it alive. Love is indeed something you do.

4

On Being in Love
and Loving

To marry without romantic, emotional involvement is ridiculous! To stay married without it is hell. As we shall see, in absolutely any marriage, you can fall in love again. We must understand the difference, however, between emotional involvement and sacrificial commitment, for if loving is something you do, romance is something you feel. While both are important, both are uniquely distinct and serve two entirely separate functions in our lives. In short, there is a vast difference between "being in love," and "loving."

"Being in love" is "those icy fingers up and down my spine, that same old witchcraft when your eyes meet mine." It is the romance of courtship and marriage, and it is fantastic. But it may not always be present. It is that which draws us together, but hardly sufficient to be that which keeps us together. "Loving" someone, however, is vastly different. It is knowing them, caring for them, hurting for them, contributing to them, a plus for a minus, a fulfillment for a need, a strength for a weakness. It is compassion and

23

kindness. "Being in love" is what you feel. "Loving" is what you do.

When two people are dating, they may find themselves falling in love. When the phone rings, his hands break out in a cold sweat and his heart asks, "Is it she?" The smell of her perfume, the fall of her hair on his chest, the touch of her hand on his, the language of the eyes which says, "I love you," when no words are spoken with the lips, is "being in love." It is fantastic, but not adequate. It is that which God gives two people which draws them together, but not that which keeps them together.

Throughout my more than twenty years of counseling, the most consistent complaint that I have heard from hundreds of married couples is, "I just don't love her anymore." The average divorce cycle goes something like this. Boy A meets girl A and "falls in love." They date two or three months or possibly six, and they marry. They do not really know each other. They have had no opportunity to learn about each other as people. They have taken none of the time necessary to search out their differences and similarities, their pluses and minuses. They have only married on their emotions.

Somewhere from six months to two years after the wedding, the sameness of the routine begins to sour the relationship, and one morning he wakes up to find out that he is no longer in love with his wife. Admit it? Perish the thought. It is unthinkable! He will live with it. Maybe it will come back. They may even take a vacation or go through a whirlwind spree of moonlight and roses all over again, but somehow the old snap is gone. Slowly the haunting thought of living with a girl that he does not love is too much for him. A year goes by or perhaps two or five, and then it happens. One day at the bottom of a depression low, she walks in. They have hired a cute new secretary at the office. Their eyes meet. Tilt! The bells ring. The birds sing. The icy fingers, the sweating palms, it is love at first sight! The secret affair, the slipping around. The wife suspects . . . the lipstick traces on the collar, the secret note is found. The confrontation, the confession, the divorce.

Now, enter girl B. Enter into wedded bliss with his refound love. At least, that is, for maybe two months or two years. No time to search out the pluses and minuses. No time to know. They met on emotion and married on emotion, and the emotions are doomed to pass. Finally, the inevitable happens. Horror of horrors, the thrill has gone. He has fallen out of love, and the cycle continues— the depression, the introduction of girl C, the affair, confrontation, the divorce. It never stops. Why? *Because we live in a culture in which love is equated with emotion.* Love is romance under the stars and violins in the moonlight. It is feeling and emotion and tingling excitment, but it knows little of compatibility, giving, sharing, blending. The answer? The first thing obviously is to understand that there is a difference between being in love and loving.

The most important thing is to expect it to happen. That's right! No marriage can be sustained by the emotional force which pulls two lovers together. Being in love will always fade. The starry-eyed romance is never the same five years after the wedding. It is inevitable; it will always happen. Healthy, mature adults must understand it and anticipate it and learn to realize that God replaces it with something far greater. Loving someone is giving to him or her, sharing a mutually beneficial blending of body and soul, mind and character, with a partner whom God has specially created for you. It is infinitely superior to teen-age crushes and fantasized infatuations with cute young secretaries! The Bible speaks of the law as being like a schoolteacher to bring us to Christ, revealing our need and pointing to Him as our sufficiency. Just so, being in love is intended to bring us to loving. How is it done?

There is no easy way really to learn to love someone. Like a stately oak, it takes time. It is not like the mushroom which appears one day and is gone the next. Not one in a hundred whirlwind romances ever consummate in the beautiful fulfillment that marriage was intended to be for two persons ideally made to "love each other." Perhaps the greatest contributing factor to divorce and marital unhappiness in our society is *the glamorized atmosphere of the dating process, the brevity of the engagement period, and the youthful age at which two persons are married.* There is just no time. How pathetic the often-heard wail of the sick marriage, "We just did not know each other."

With many couples 90 percent of the teen-age dating hours are spent looking at movies and listening to rock records. To suggest to most young people that they spend a quiet evening at home, seated on a couch or in a swing in the back yard, talking to each other about themselves or about life would to them be to suggest a fate worse than death. They take no time to talk, no time to know each other. They are living on emotion in a whirlwind of fantasy. One day they will crash and crash hard.

Many people wake up too late to the fact that they are married to someone they never really knew. While I do not suggest such a drastic and radical extreme, I learned in Ireland when visiting there in 1959 that the average engagement was from two to nine years. The average marrying age was twenty-seven for women and thirty for men. And the average divorce rate was one in one hundred. What a contrast to the fantasy world of American romance, where most date three to six months, marry in their teens, and one-half divorce in two to ten years.

What of you who are already married? What has this to do with you? Very much, indeed! If your marriage is in this condition, there is help for you too. The fact of life is that people do not remain "in love" forever. Emotional romance always fades. But God replaces it with something far superior if you will take the time with His help to probe, to search, to talk, to give, to blend. It is hard to believe that "loving" can be better than "being in love," but if you will work at it, you will find that it is.

During courtship the pluses tend to come to the surface. We are the aggressor, the pursuer. We are working at it, constantly on our good behavior. We put our best foot forward to impress, to woo, and to win. Courtship tends to bring out the best in us, but marriage tends to bring about the worst in us! Then we let down. The conquest is over. The thrill of the chase is gone. For the shallow-of-spirit, the pleasure of the pursuit has dimmed the satisfaction of the possession, and there are no fields left to conquer, no hands left to win. So we give up and let up. With our defenses down, the worst in us begins to surface, and those minuses come quickly to the top. They start to clash against powerful pluses, and divorce often appears to be the only solution. But take hope, for you can fall in love again.

5

You Can Fall in
Love Again

I am going to share something fantastic with you in this chapter. Something you will read nowhere else. I have never heard or read a word on it in print by preacher, psychologist, or counselor. How tragic that the most often recurring problem in marriage has been the least explored. If there is a vast difference between being in love and loving someone, it is equally true as it is normal that we crave still to be "in love."

Years ago people began coming to me with marital problems. Ninety percent of them have been married from two to seven years, though some have been married as long as thirty.

In the movie that made Marilyn Monroe famous, *The Seven Year Itch,* the idea was that about every seven years most married people begin to itch where they can't scratch. They know something is wrong, but they don't know what. Usually they have an affair around that time. I think the writer of Miss Monroe's movie was nearer to the truth than he might have known. Of the six basic categories of marital problems, that which has by far arisen the most often is, "I just don't love her anymore."

I have heard it in hard, serious counseling sessions more than a thousand times. And so I began to do what any counselor would, study, research, and read. To my amazement, I made a shocking discovery: To my knowledge not one word from any author has ever been written on this tremendously important subject. No minister could advise me. No psychologist, direct me. No researcher's information could enlighten me; so God alone would have to help. Because I have always believed that within the pages of the Bible lie the answers to all of life's problems, I began to search there for the answer.

At last I found it in the final book of the Bible, in chapter two of the Book of Revelation:

Unto the angel of the church of Ephesus write; These things saith he that holdeth the seven stars in his right hand, who walketh in the midst of the seven golden candlesticks;
I know thy works, and thy labour, and thy patience, and how thou canst not bear them which are evil: and thou hast tried them which say they are apostles, and are not, and hast found them liars: And hast borne, and hast patience, and for my name's sake hast laboured, and hast not fainted. Nevertheless I have somewhat against thee, because thou hast left thy first love. Remember therefore from whence thou art fallen, and repent, and do the first works; or else I will come unto thee quickly, and will remove thy candlestick out of his place, except thou repent.

Revelation 2:1–5

30

Jesus Christ, the heavenly Bridegroom, is dictating a letter through the Apostle John to His bride, the church at Ephesus.

In the first verse He reminds her who He is, the glorious Son of God, Creator of the world, Upholder of the law. He says that He has not changed through eternity; He is to her as He has always been. In verses two and three He commends her for her fidelity to Him, for her work, her patience, her disgust at evil, her doctrinal integrity, and her consistent effort in His behalf. At the beginning of the fourth verse, however, the whole tenor of the conversation begins to change. "Nevertheless I have somewhat against thee, because thou hast left thy first love." Her love for the groom has slipped. It is not the vibrant thing it once was. She has fallen out of love. How will the loving bridegroom, the master marital authority, deal with the problem?

The first overtones of the fourth verse give a surprising subtle hint as to what will be His approach. He is understanding, He is patient, and yet He is upset. It is not a light thing! A grevious wrong has been done, and He will deal with it directly and rather severely. "Nevertheless I have somewhat against thee, because thou hast left thy first love." *I have something against thee!* I am charging you with a serious offense. This expression, "against thee," is heavy terminology. It is a serious charge but not one without remedy. In the fifth verse He gives His perfect three-point prescription on how to fall in love again.

LOVE IS SOMETHING YOU DO

(1) Remember
(2) Repent
(3) Do

1. REMEMBER

"Remember from whence thou art fallen." Remember the bliss of the early marital state. The mind can be a powerful ally or an awesome enemy. Sometimes people come to me and say, "I've been thinking about divorce." That kind of thinking will get you in trouble! "As a man thinketh in his heart, so is he." When we keep an image in our mind, everything within us tends to gravitate toward its realization. If we think failure, we will fail. If we think success, we can succeed.

The first part of Jesus' prescription to the loveless bride is to enlist all the power of the mind as an ally in her effort to regain lost love. Remember that you have loved this man and that it is possible for you to love him again. You have loved him in the past, and therefore it does lie in the realm of possibility to love him. It is not a nonexistent thing. It has been done. It has already been accomplished and experienced, and what has been done can be done again. Go ahead, admit it. Make yourself say it. Say it again and again. "I can love this person. I *have* loved him. I have done it, and it is possible for me to do it again."

Sometimes people say, "Well, I guess I never really loved her at all." Not so! You know you loved her or you would not have married her in the first place. You loved her at the time. You loved her before you married her, when you married her and for at least a time after you married her. Eliminate those negative thoughts by focusing on positive ones. The positive thinker does not refuse to acknowledge the negative; he merely refuses to dwell on it.

The New Testament writers were teaching positive thinking long before this generation ever heard of it. "Finally, brethren, whatsoever things are true, whatsoever things are honest, whatsoever things are just, whatsoever things are pure, whatsoever things are lovely, whatsoever things are of good report; if there by any virtue, and if there be any praise, think on these things. Those things, which ye have both learned and received, and heard, and seen in me, do: and the God of peace shall be with you. But I rejoiced in the Lord greatly, that now at the last your care of me hath flourished again; wherein ye were also careful, but ye lacked opportunity. Not that I speak in respect of want: for I have learned, in whatsoever state I am, therewith to be content" (Phil. 4:8–11). That's good, positive thinking, and Jesus commands it as a part of His prescription for falling in love again.

Relive every word, every incident, every kiss, every touch as you were falling in love and dating this person you once loved. Remember the wedding moment by moment, flower by flower, promise by promise; remember the joy as you drove away from the church, the joy of your wedding night, the esctasy of the honeymoon. Remember that first apartment, the first time you went grocery shopping together. Remember all over, again and again in your mind. Remember how you felt, all of your hopes and dreams. Focus on that, and there will come gradually to your heart the desire to relive it, to pick up the pieces of a broken love affair and love again. Remember that state from whence you are fallen. Remember that once you loved.

2. REPENT

What a shock it was for me to find the command to repent as the second ingredient in Jesus' three-part prescription for falling in love again, but it is there without amplification or explanation. The other two words are supported by "remember the state from whence thou art fallen" and "do the first works again." But this word *repent* stands alone. He simply says, "And repent." Now we begin to see why Jesus approached the subject in such a severe way when He said to His bride, "I have somewhat against thee," because she had left her first love (Himself). He is treating the matter as a spiritual problem. Surprisingly He deals with it as a sin, for only a sin can be repented of.

Why does Jesus say such a thing as repent? Why is falling out of love dealt with in part as a sin? It can only be because falling out of love is a symptom of a spiritual malady. If God is love and the author of love, and God alone can give real love, then when the process of the integration of the selfless meshing of two personalities has begun to collapse, it is because *agape* love is gone. God's love has departed because God was not wanted.

Where He is not invited, He will not go. Since the day Jesus was born in a stable, He has proved He only moves into those places which we vacate for Him. Perfect, selfless love, then, is an exclusive attribute of God's presence in the human heart, and when that goes, the capacity to love goes with it. It is the symptom of a spiritual problem.

To fall in love again you must be absolutely honest with yourself and go back to your relationship with God. Where did you jump the track? When did you first begin to fall out of love with Him? When did your heart first begin to grow cold? You will usually be able to trace your lack of love for your husband or wife to a very short time after the beginning of your loss of love for the Lord. The hardest thing you may ever do is to ask heavenly forgiveness for the sin of falling out of love. But it is an essential ingredient of the prescription, and one without which it absolutely will not work. Go ahead, 'fess up, come clean with God. Admit it. When His love begins again to flow into you, then it will be able to flow out of you.

How pathetic it is to counsel with young people who are about to be married, who have made plans for their job, apartment, automobile, but have given no attention to their spiritual relationship. Marriage is a divine institution. The meshing of two personalities is a miracle from heaven which can only be maximized as they are oiled by the Spirit of God. Our religious faith is no option. It is the essence of the marriage relationship. Where you work and where you live are relatively unimportant, but Jesus living in your heart is the one thing that makes it all go. His love overflows to others. Without Him the marriage relationship may very often be reduced to a shriveled and dying thing.

Before we turn to the third ingredient of the prescription, we would do well to take a brief look at the biblical ramifications of the expression "to repent." Three things are involved in religious repentance.

A change of *attitude,* and change of *direction,* and a change of *mind.* To confess is to admit to God, to yourself, and to your partner that you are wrong and verbally to ask their forgiveness. Repentance entails a change of attitude that leads to contrition and sorrow, mental acknowledgement and a broken heart. No broken heart ever came to His feet in humility and contrition that did not find the troubled waters of a turbulent spirit immediately calmed by His gentle "peace be still." All you have to do is to offer Him your brokenness and sorrow, and He will do the rest.

Then, too, biblical repentance entails a change of direction. It means to get back on the track and start doing again what you were doing. Get back in church, back in the mainstream, where spiritual growth occurs. We may be assured that His promise is secure, that "if we confess our sins, he is faithful and just to forgive us our sins and to cleanse us from all unrighteousness."

3. "AND DO THE FIRST WORKS"

First, He has told us to use the mind, to remember the first state, to remember how it was when we were in love. Second, we are to use the heart to repent. Third He commands that the body be used as an ally of the mind, not only to remember how we acted, but also to start acting in the same way again. To "do again" is the clear requirement of this part of the prescription. Some of you are probably saying, "Do you mean that I am to play a game, to put on an act, to respond where I am unresponsive, to say what I do not mean and do what I do not really feel?" The answer is an emphatic *yes*.

What happens psychologically and therapeutically in the process in which the mind addresses the self, the soul addresses the Lord, and the bodily actions address the injured marital partner? As the totality of one's being is thrust into the role of rebuilding the broken relationship, the one who is now acting will find two phases in the response of his spouse. The first will probably be suspicion. If you are the one that has not fallen out of love and you see that your partner is trying his best to follow the prescription for falling in love again, whatever else you do, let him play the game. You must be neither suspicious, accusative, or condemnatory. Whatever you do, don't say, "You are just pretending." For heaven's sake, let him do it and be grateful that he cares enough to try!

The second phase will be your partner's response to the new you. He will become a new person and you can love the new him. If a relationship has grown sour, then neither party is *acting* as once he or she did. They are both only *reacting*. A chicken-egg cycle occurs to which there is no solution. Someone must make a start, somebody has to take the iniative to break the cycle, and this is where you begin. Much has been written on the power of the mind to assist the will in thinking one's way to new action; but the plain teaching of Jesus, the Master Psychologist, is that it is far easier to act one's way to new thinking.

"I do not love my wife or my husband. Therefore, we do not enjoy sex or companionship, and so on. I cannot kiss him. I do not like to be with him. I do not want to live in the same room with him. I can't stand for him to touch me." Every marriage counselor has heard it a hundred times. What are these people saying? They are saying that I do not *feel* something, therefore, I cannot *do* something. They are saying if I *felt* a certain way, if I were "in love" with him, then I could *act* a certain way. Jesus is saying that if you *act* a certain way, then you will *feel* a certain way. The game must be played. The act must be initiated and the pretense kept up.

Obviously this is a hard part of the prescription. But don't waste your time looking for another book, from another doctor, with another answer. There is no other prescription. This is a one-treatment disease. There is only one thing that works and this is it. It is a medicine with three ingredients and you have just read its label of contents. *There are no exceptions. Nothing else works. If you add anything to it or take anything from it, it will fail.*

Only in recent years did I learn this prescription. I have probably shared it with four hundred couples. Only about one-fourth of them agreed without exception or variance to follow it implicitly. Absolutely everyone of those couples have fallen in love again—affectionately, erotically, romantically, emotionally in love again. The others didn't think it worth the trouble. It is a tough prescription and one that must be absolutely and implicitly followed to the last detail without exception if it is to work.

Is it worth it to you? Is the salvation of your home, the stability of your children, the sacredness of your commitment, and the sanctity of your own well-being worth the effort? No one can answer that question but you. You *can* fall in love again, but the medicine is hard to take. The prescription is tough, but it works if you think it is worth it.

6

When You Have
to Forgive

Then came Peter to him, and said, Lord, how oft shall my brother sin against me, and I forgive him? till seven times? Jesus saith unto him, I say not unto thee, Until seven times: but, Until seventy times seven.

Therefore is the kingdom of heaven likened unto a certain king, which would take account of his servants. And when he had begun to reckon, one was brought unto him, which owed him ten thousand talents. But forasmuch as he had not to pay, his lord commanded him to be sold, and his wife, and children, and all that he had, and payment to be made. The servant therefore fell down, and worshipped him, saying, Lord, have patience with me, and I will pay thee all. Then the lord of that servant was moved with compassion, and loosed him, and forgave him the debt. But the same servant went out, and found one of his fellowservants, which owed him an hundred pence: and he laid hands on him, and took him by the throat, saying, Pay me that thou owest. And his fellowservant fell down at his feet, and besought him, saying, Have patience with me, and I will pay thee all. And he would not: but went and cast him into prison, till he should pay the debt. So when his fellowservants saw what was done, they were very sorry, and came and told unto their lord all that was done. Then his lord, after that he had called him, said unto him, O thou wicked servant, I forgave thee all that debt, because thou desiredst me: Shouldest not thou also have had compassion on thy fellowservant, even as I had pity on thee? And his lord was wroth, and delivered him to the tormentors, till he should pay all that was due unto him. So likewise shall my heavenly Father do also unto you, if ye from your hearts forgive not every one his brother their trespasses.

Matthew 18:21–35

At the height of the war between the Armenians and Turks, a young Armenian girl and her brother, a young soldier, were captured by a Turkish soldier who raped the girl and killed her brother before her eyes. Later she escaped and became a nurse in the Armenian army and was assigned the responsibility of caring for wounded Turkish soldiers. One day the young Turk was brought to her hospital at the point of death. She looked into his eyes and realized that with the slightest neglect she could let him die and even the score. But she didn't! Meticulously she nursed him back to health. When he was stronger, he asked, "You know who I am, don't you?"

"Yes," she replied.

"Why, then have you done this to me when you could have let me die?"

Quietly she responded, "It is because I have a religion that teaches me to forgive my enemies." Indeed we have just such a religion. The Christian faith is unique in that it alone has a doctrine of forgiveness. Sometimes your mate will be untrue. Sometimes you have to forgive.

We owe much to Simon Peter with his quick tongue, for I think he often drew from Jesus His best insights about life. One day he asked Jesus, "How many times should a man forgive his brother? Seven times?" In so saying, Peter thought that he had demonstrated to Jesus his understanding of Christian grace. The rabbinical teaching stated that if a man sinned against you once, he was to be forgiven, and the second time as well. If he sinned against you three times, you forgave him again. But if he sinned the fourth time, you did not forgive. Three was the human limitation for forgiveness. Peter decided to double the amount and throw in one for good measure! But Jesus said, "No, Peter, I say unto you not unto seven times do you forgive your brother who sins against you, but until seventy times seven."

Jesus was not really placing a limitation of 490 on forgiveness. He was trying instead to teach Peter that he could not reduce the concept of grace to a mere system of legal ethics. Rather, that it is, in essence, limitless. The entire thesis of the doctrine of Christian forgiveness is simply that so much greater are the transgressions that have been forgiven us that the only way we can receive forgiveness of God is ourselves to forgive those who sin against us. Let me emphasize that again. Jesus has plainly and distinctly said that a man cannot receive forgiveness from God unless and until he is willing to forgive others. That which has been forgiven us by God is so infinitely greater than anything we could forgive another human being who has sinned against us that it is ridiculous by comparison.

Jesus said here is a man who is owed a very small debt, but he himself has been forgiven a debt of ten thousand talents. Ten thousand talents is the equivalent of more than eight million dollars. He fell down before his master and said, "Lord, I cannot pay the eight million dollars. Don't cast me into prison, please forgive me the debt. Don't take my wife, don't take my children. Please, please forgive." The master's heart was moved with compassion, and he canceled the debt. Then this very same man finds his fellow servant who owed him seventeen dollars, who in turn pleads to be released from his debt. But he refused to forgive him and cast him into jail. When the other servants saw what had happened, they went to the master and said that the man to whom he had forgiven the eight-million-dollar debt would not forgive the debt of a man who owed him seventeen dollars. The master was filled with anger and cast the servant into prison. Jesus said just so does your heavenly Father deal with you.

This is a serious teaching. You cannot be forgiven of your sins until you forgive other people. It is the plain teaching of the gospel, and it is severe and restrictive. Jesus is saying that there is nothing that another sinner can do against us who are also sinners to compare with what we have done against God.

Why? For one thing, because we have sinned against innocence, against one who is holy. We have sinned against one who cannot sin against us. Oh, the unfathomable concept of Christian grace! No wonder it is called "amazing grace."

Not only does He who has never sinned forgive the debt, but He comes to us and searches us out and pleads with us to accept His forgiveness. So great is His grace that it is unthinkable to God that a forgiven sinner would fail to forgive another sinner.

Therefore, Jesus teaches that the forgiveness of God becomes conditional upon our forgiveness of others. Now notice that I did not say that our forgiveness of other people is conditional, but that the forgiveness of God is conditional upon our forgiveness of other people. The Christian gospel teaches that our forgiveness of other people is not conditional. Jesus did not say you are to forgive a man if he asks you to forgive him. He did not say you are to forgive a man if he deserves to be forgiven or even if he wants that forgiveness. He does not say you are to forgive your unfaithful husband or wife because he or she has repented and asked your forgiveness. He said that forgiveness is absolutely unconditional. You don't forgive him because he wants it or because he asks for it or deserves it. You forgive because as Christian husbands and wives it is our nature to forgive.

Why did Jesus put this condition upon our being forgiven of God? I think because there is so little forgiveness on the human level that it is hard for us to believe that God really forgives. God wants our help in being able visually to get across to the world that forgiveness is a reality. Someone has said that probably 90 percent of the people in mental institutions could be healed if they truly believed that God forgives them.

Jesus says act it out, live it out, demonstrate it.

It becomes, then, a command, a requirement of our own forgiveness. People say to me sometime, "I can forgive, but I can't forget." Nonsense! Some of you forget very well. You have forgotten the last twenty good things your husband or your wife did for you because you can only remember the one bad thing he or she did ten years ago. We tend to remember what we want to remember and forget what we want to forget.

Jesus' teaching on forgiveness is something like an automobile. You dare not run your car on steel rims with no rubber tires, or electricity may come into it and kill you. But with rubber tires the car is insulated and electricity cannot flow out of you; so it will not flow into you. If it can't get out of the car, it can't get into the car. And if forgiveness can't get out of you, it is not going to get into you. Forgiveness is a requirement of God that is unalterable. It is the plain teaching of our Lord Jesus and has never been revoked. Where there is unforgiveness, there will be no grace flowing into the soul of a marriage. Did not our Lord in His model prayer say that every time we pray for the forgiveness of our sins, we must in the same breath add, "As we forgive those who sinned against us."

In Alfred Lord Tennyson's immortal story of King Arthur, the king had gone away on a long trip and Lady Guinevere had been unfaithful and had an affair with handsome Sir Lancelot. Upon his return he learns the news, and soon she is divorced and put away. Down toward the end of her life and the end of the story, he goes to see her in a convent where she is now at the point of death. At the close of his beautiful soliloquy he says, "But, lo, I forgive thee even as eternal God forgives," and walks away. Beautiful poetry, but *atrocious theology.* Had he forgiven her as Eternal God forgives, he would have taken her out of the convent, brought her back home, put regal robes on her back, and, as the prodigal, reinstated her to her place on the throne, stuck out his hand to Sir Lancelot, and said, "I forgive you. You are still my friend." *That is forgiveness.* That is the way eternal God forgives. He doesn't leave broken-hearted sinners in convents of despair. *Agape* love forgives, forgets, and reinstates.

When you have to forgive, you do just that. *Have* to forgive, and you can!

7

The Bed Undefiled

The contemporary layman is often shocked to read the old theologians and repeatedly find the expression "intercourse with God." It described the intimate relationship of the *Blessed Presence in the life of the believer* but can hardly be used in good taste today. Yet the idea that it was meant to convey is not only a perfect description of the most intimate of heavenly relationships, but one that God chose to use Himself.

The most heavenly of human relationships is the union, the intercourse, of two personalities who love each other. Today we use a single word *love* to describe many of life's relations. The broader, fuller Greek language, however, uses three words: *agape,* God's heavenly love for us; *phileo,* meaning "brotherly love," from which we get the word *Philadelphia; eros,* the romantic and sexual love of a man for a woman, from which comes the term *erotic.*

The Apostle Paul brings his Letter to the Hebrews to a conclusion with a broad sweep of life's relationships of love.

LOVE IS SOMETHING YOU DO

Verse 1. Love your brothers.
Verse 2. Love strangers.
Verse 3. Love the prisoners.
Verse 4. Love your spouse.
Verse 5. Love life.
Verse 6. Love the Lord.
Verse 7. Love your leaders.
Verse 8. Love Jesus Christ.
Verse 9. Love the Word.

In the fourth verse, his brief treatise on marriage, he employs the ancient antiphonal device of contrast for emphasis. "Marriage is honorable in all, and the bed undefiled: but whoremongers and adulterers God will judge" (Heb. 13:4). The sainted Apostle, as does his Lord, has much to say about marriage. In this particular passage, however, he speaks only of the binding nature of the sexual union and the sacred blessing pronounced upon it by God.

The marriage bed is undefiled, that is, it is holy, right, heaven blessed. God's very purpose in His involvement in the affairs of man is to indwell man, to be inside of him, to live within him, the two becoming one, that He might fulfill him and give him life. All believers have a marriage-type relationship with the Father, an "intercourse" with the Divine.

In the Scriptures, believers are referred to by three symbolisms:

(1) As the church in living union with her Lord.
(2) As the body on earth joined to the head in heaven.
(3) As the bride of Christ who is her groom.

48

"Wives, submit yourselves unto your own husbands, as unto the Lord. For the husband is the head of the wife, even as Christ is the head of the church: and He is the Saviour of the body" (Eph. 5:22–23).

As a part of the church, the believer is the dwelling place in which the Spirit of God tabernacles in a human body. He is her Lord. He indwells her, possesses her, fulfills her. Just so, by the very nature of the sex act, the wife is fulfilled by her husband; she opens her body to his, she receives and contains him, his life flows into hers and fills her being as does God his own. As the body, we cannot exist apart from the head. The head fills, creates, dreams, and loves, but what is the head without the body? Through the body love is expressed, the dream fulfilled. Nor can the head live apart from the body, for all of its capacities are mute, all of its powers latent, unless the brain and nerves and emotions find fulfillment through its organs and limbs. As the heavenly Bridegroom pours Himself into His bride, the church, so does the husband fulfill his bride, but the simile is even more extensive.

Think first of the courtship, the heavenly romance, when first the Spirit of God seeks out the believer to be His bride. He woos her, charms her, loves her, and wins her; but all the romance and intent are for naught unless there is the response of commitment. When two persons stand before the minister and respond to the question, Do you take this man or woman to be your wedded husband or wife? everything is at stake—all of the courtship, the dreams, the intentions, everything. By one simple "I do" or "I do not" the future is sealed.

One does not come into vital union with the Lord Jesus by the process of spiritual osmosis. There must be a moment of conversion, a point of commitment, an in-time, in-place specific yielding in which the wooed believer says the eternal "I do" to the heavenly Lover. Friends are invited to the public testimony of the ceremony. The wedding ring has no power to unite; but it is symbolic of the union just as baptism symbolizes the beginning of the public declaration of intent. The honeymoon is the first full taste of new wine, the first full blush of the ecstasy of one body, one soul, one being, one life. And such is the joy of the new convert.

What is born of that union? As children, made in the image of the parents, are born, so the believer, possessed by the heavenly Lover, will likewise bring forth His spiritual fruit. Spiritual children will be born and the circle continued and completed.

With the eyes, a man loves. With his brain, he thinks. With his mind, he understands. With his heart, he feels. With his being, he intends. With his soul, he commits. But what is a head without the body? And what is a man without his bride? Where then is the focus of the funnel, the zenith of expression? It is often said erroneously that every nerve from the brain focuses through the spinal column and to the base of the spine, but such is not the case. In the physical anatomy of both men and women the base of their being continues through the trunk of nerves which flow to the tip of the sexual organ. There, at its point, comes to flow the entirety of all the drive, desire, nerve, power, and emotion that makes us at once divinely human and humanly divine, earthly beings made in the image of the heavenly.

The sexual intercourse of man and wife consummates the totality of being, the blending of soul, the union of two spirits. The twain become one flesh as the woman opens her being to her husband and as he possesses and indwells her; they are one spirit, one soul, one being. This gorgeous and heavenly consummation of two beings created by God for each other, ordained to be one flesh, one soul, one being, is the ultimate expression of flow into oneness. It is honorable in all things—heavenly, precious, and sacred, to be lifted above the vulgar, the obscene, the animalistic into the holy and the heavenly and "The Bed Undefiled."

A sexual relationship outside the bond of Christian marriage is not simply wrong because God forbids it, though that would be sufficient. God forbids it because it is wrong, and it is wrong because it cheats and steals and robs people of the best. Sex for sex' sake, the mere physical gratification of the genitals, is no relationship at all. Sex cannot exist apart from the whole.

Sex for the woman demands security. It requires that she give the soul of her being to the man and, that she entrust her body to his possessiveness and control. In sexual intercourse, not just her body, but everything in her cries out for his control. Her body is comprised of brains and nerves and emotions and needs and psyche. Her heart and soul are saying, "Care for me, protect me, provide for my children, secure my future, feed my stomach, pay my bills, meet all my needs."

Sex for the man demands a corresponding responsibility. When he possesses a woman, all of his being is saying, "I will be your defense, I will be your shield, I will be your hero, I will provide for you, for all of you, for everything that there is in you." Apart from the bond of marriage, the deepest emotional and psychological needs of human beings cannot be met, and the defiled bed is no bed at all. Sex without commitment, a commitment possible only in the bond of marriage, is only a microscopic percentage of the total blending of personalities. Sex therefore is only a part and an expression. Sex outside of marriage makes a promise it cannot fulfill and cries for a responsibility it cannot accept, while demanding security that it cannot provide.

Where there is no permanent commitment, there is no satisfaction. There is only trauma, guilt, and frustration. This sort of guilt and frustration is not induced by some Victorian shiboleth or Puritanical code of antiquated morality; it is produced because it is possible to produce nothing else. Spirit, mind, soul, emotions, security, need, everything that makes us divinely human is expressed sexually, and that is not simply the message of the church. It is a fact of life, the plan of the Divine. It is, as surely as the sun rises in the east and sets in the west, the way it is! Adultery is not wrong simply because God forbids it; it is

wrong because it is a cheap substitute, a fraud, **an**d a fake. It promises what it cannot produce, **an**d it creates a need it cannot fulfill. Adultery is **a** gip and a cheat, and God does not want people **to** be gipped and get hurt. His laws are negative **an**d positive. His "thou shalts" and "thou shalt **no**ts" are to protect us and to preserve and guard **fo**r us the best.

Sex in marriage between two persons is the ulti-mate, divine, ecstatic, unspeakable expression of **the** totality of being, and it is sanctified by God. So **far** is it from being the bed defiled that while, not **the** only thing in marriage, it is certainly the focal **un**ion of everything that is marriage. Marriage, therefore, is honorable in all things, "The Bed Un-defiled."

8

Sex—the Unselfish Gift

Every serious adult should understand the similarities and the differences between the male and the female sex drive. At puberty, the adolescent male first becomes aware of the dawning of the dynamic sexual force that resides in his body. And this physical development proceeds far more quickly than his emotions are equipped to handle. Normally several alternatives present themselves —some good, some less than perfect. Masturbation, wet dreams, sexual fantasies, projection, sublimation, and fornication are ready outlets to a difficult problem. Easy access to pornographic material provides a simple though pathetic resolution for many. Guilt and frustration follow. Depression, self-recrimination, fear of discovery, real or imagined sexual inadequacy normally follow, for regardless of his understanding, or lack of it, of how to deal with the matter, one thing is painfully true: the powerful sex drive of a young man has reached the zenith of its force in his late teen-age years and early twenties. From about ages seventeen to twenty-three, the male sex drive peaks. From then until death, but ever so slowly, it diminishes but never fully dies. Even the very elderly, into their eighties and nineties, often have a vital sexual vibrancy.

The sexual physiology of the female is in marked contrast to the male. Her body ripens long before her sexual drive is correspondingly awakened. When she is fifteen, sixteen, and seventeen, she may be very beautiful and sexually attractive; but though she is highly desirable sexually to a man, her own sexual awareness is only beginning to awaken. Not until her twenties will she begin to blossom into fullness and peak at a much longer lasting plateau throughout her thirties and only gradually begin to diminish in her early forties.

A teen-age girl is attractive to a man, but there is little corresponding sexual pull toward him on her part. She is mostly curious about his body, and she is flattered at his interest. This sort of flattery can make an insecure girl very easy prey for the advances of a man who in reality has no interest in her other than a sexual one. Her body is much more interesting to him than is his to her. She does not find his bony, hairy legs particularly sexy! She does not stand in front of the newsstands and gaze at pictures of the male body. The male and female are different.

The female sex drive begins later, runs deeper, entails more commitment, and lasts longer. While a man may proceed through sex to love, women— real women—proceed through love to sex and cannot find fulfillment for the deepest longings of their feminine being except cradled in the nest of true commitment and security. Why the difference?

In my twenty years of marriage counseling, I have found that there are six common areas of difficulty in marriage:

> (1) Falling out of love
> (2) Relatives
> (3) Religion
> (4) Money
> (5) Communication
> (6) Sex

In my opinion there should never be any problem in sex. There is no need for engaged couples to experiment; in most cases any two persons can be sexually compatible. Someone has well said that there are really no frigid wives—there are only ignorant husbands. But obviously there are psychologically frigid women; so why problems in sex? Because the male is introduced early in life to a very real and vital problem—a sex drive with no seeming legitimate outlet. Thus he begins to turn within himself and in his fantasy, sublimation, and projections begins to deal with his sex drive as best he can. By the time he marries, he has often developed gross misconceptions about sexuality. The woman is the long-desired object of his sexual frustration; she is *his* fulfillment, *his* satisfaction, *his* pleasure, *his* prize. Sex has become selfish, and the woman becomes unsatisfied. She may experience orgasm, but she is deeply aware that something in her feminine psyche is unsatisfied. Her body has been fulfilled, but not her heart and soul. A strong male self-centeredness is obvious in the foreplay, or lack of it, in the approach, and in the act of intercourse itself. Gentleness and patience, the words, the consideration are nonexistent. Mere biological sexual satisfaction does not necessarily guarantee the fulfillment of her feminine psyche. A young man's sex drive is more powerful than a young woman's, demands more satisfaction, more attention, more often. She smiles, she responds, and in a very real sense she is often sexually satisfied; but there is something that she does not understand, that she cannot explain. Something is definitely missing.

Through the years she plays the game, she pretends. During his thirties, the husband often becomes greatly interested in his business, in his own self-image, in his self-worth and accomplishment. Preoccupied with the desire to get ahead and fatigued in body and mind, he begins to slip sexually. As with the femininity of the woman, so the whole masculinity of the male is involved with a healthy ego structure. A man cannot think well of himself if he does not feel that he is sexually adequate, for his entire masculinity, hence, his ego structure, is threatened. He may turn to affair after affair or to sublimation or projection, conquering first this business and then that problem to prove himself to himself. The woman simultaneously is becoming increasingly aware that her own sexuality is beginning to broaden and deepen and her capacity to love, to give all of herself—all of her real being—has begun to climax simultaneously with her husband's sexual demise. Frustration upon frustration caves in upon them both, and spiritual, emotional, and psychological help is desperately needed.

Why all of this? Why did God create us so that the man's sex drive peaks in his late teens and early twenties and the woman's from the mid-twenties to the thirties and into the early forties? Why didn't God create us so that two people are both at the peak of their sexual potency at age twenty-one and experience a perfect parallel of the sexual drive until death? The answer is a simple and beautiful one: *because sex would then be selfish. God has created us so that at any given time in their lives, sexual fulfillment comes more quickly and more easily for one partner than for the other, so that at any given time in their lives, one partner must always be thinking more of the fulfillment of the other than of himself.* Sex, then, is lifted from biological gratification of the self to the totally emotional and spiritual level that is the heavenly fulfillment designed and intended by the Creator. To experience sex—perfect, holy, beautiful, Christian marital sexual relationships —*is not simply to get, but to give.* Never is the ultimate ecstasy of sex experienced until, like the beautiful heavenly gift of Himself in love to His bride, the church, sex is experienced in an atmosphere of *selflessness.*

As in all heavenly things, we receive by giving. The unique distinction of our Christian faith is that what is sacrificed, what is given away in Christlike selflessness, is given again to us—lifted, enhanced, sanctified. The ultimate pleasure and deepest satisfaction of sex is not the physical gratification of the self but the fulfillment of the marriage partner. This ultimate satisfaction cannot be experienced in the backseat of automobiles by teen-agers who are going steady, or by a man having an affair with his secretary. It is experienced in the selfless, spiritual, mature nest of security and responsibility and Christian selflessness which dies to itself that the other might live.

In the sperm of the male, there is life-giving power. When life is given to another, a sense of new life is miraculously experienced in the being of the giver. Jesus said, "He that loseth his life for my sake shall find it." And the Apostle Paul added, "Wives, submit yourselves unto your own husbands, as unto the Lord. . . . Husbands, love your wives, even as Christ also loved the church, and gave Himself for it." How did Jesus earn the undying love which gains Him the right to indwell and possess the life of His bride? By selflessly dying for her on the cross, by dying that she might live, by giving that she might receive. And, husbands, wives will only be too happy to love and honor you as their lord, their controller, their possessor when you give yourself to them unselfishly as Christ gave Himself for His bride, the church.

Remember, you cannot outgive Him. You give Him 10 percent of your income, and you don't end up with 90 percent. You end up with 120 percent or 150 percent of the original. You give Him a day a week; He does not give you back six. He gives you eight or ten. The symbol for Christianity is the cross—an *I* crossed out. Dying, sacrificing, giving, but a giving which ended in death? No, a thousand times no! It is the planting to receive again,

a giving to receive, an offering of life's relationships to be made holy, to be sanctified. It is a Cal-
vary before Easter. In giving we shall receive; in
dying we shall live.

Two people with a perfect paralleling sex
drive? What a dismal thought! How insipid! How
tasteless the love life! But He created us so that
one must always be patient, restrained, self-sac-
rificing, preoccupied with the pleasure, the fulfillment of the other, and then sex is glorious! Then
it is honorable in all things—and the bed undefiled.

Romantic love lifted into *agape* love becomes
heavenly love—ecstatic as you have never known
—because it is selfless, because it lifts. And that is
why an all-wise and wonderful God created us as
He did. The enhancing and intensifying of one's
own feeling in response to the simultaneous orgasm of the partner is so beyond that of solitary
orgasm as to be undescribable. Selfless sex is
heavenly sex, and that is why our sex drives peak
at different ages. To give is to receive. It is the
essence of our faith, and the fact of life of the
sexual relationship.

9

The Forbidden Fruit

Jesus said, "Are ye also yet without understanding? Do not ye yet understand, that whatsoever
entereth in at the mouth goeth into the belly, and
is cast out into the draught? But those things
which proceed out of the mouth come forth from
the heart; and they defile the man. For out of the
heart proceed evil thoughts, murders, adulteries,
fornications, thefts, false witness, blasphemies"
(Matt. 15:16–19). In this passage Jesus suggests
three categories of evil which defile a man. To
each category there is a common denominator—
taking what is not rightfully yours.

There is first that which a man steals from another man. Jesus gives three illustrations of what
a man steals from another man and thus defiles
himself. For one thing, He mentions stealing
physical things. He says you defile yourself because you commit thievery, by taking a physical
object from someone else. I don't know when, if
ever, I have heard a sermon on the downright
meanery of stealing. I think it needs to be said,
and it needs to be said often. On a recent night the
home of the minister of music of our church was

robbed, and many valuable possessions were stolen. It is an awful thing to think of someone in
your car, in your home, in your possessions.
Hardly a week goes by that something is not stolen
or pilfered from our church building. People have
slept there overnight to rob us from the inside. It
is an awful thing for a man to have the audacity
tangibly to take something from someone that
doesn't belong to him. It is so awful that Jesus
Christ warned that the person who is a thief defiles himself.

In our day sin is glossed over and excused. Men
call acts of sin accidents; God calls sin abomina-
tion. Men call sin a blunder; God calls sin blind-
ness. Men call sin a defect; God calls it a disease.
Men call sin an error; God calls it enmity. Men call
sin a chance; God calls it a choice. Men call sin a
fascination; God calls it a fatality. Men call sin an
infirmity; God calls it iniquity. Jesus says that one
of the things that defiles a man is to take the
physical possession that belongs to another.

But there is something else that falls under the
category of taking from another man that which
is not rightfully yours, and that is taking his life,
murder. The Commandments say, "Thou shalt
not kill," that is, thou shalt do no murder. It is an
awful thing for a man to murder, but there is a
difference between killing and murder. Murder is
hatred in the heart, malice. A soldier may kill
because he has to, because it is a responsibility;
but he doesn't necessarily kill because he hates.
What's in the heart is the thing. It is so awful to
hate a man in your heart that Jesus says that you
have as good as killed him if you hate him. By far,

that is worse than a man who doesn't hate but kills because he has to. But Jesus said there is another kind of killing. There is another way of taking something from a man that is far worse than taking his physical possession or taking his life. There is a kind of thievery that occurs when there is a false witness. When you steal from a man his reputation, his standing in the community, the respect of his family, his job, his good name by lying against him, you have taken far more than when you take his life. It is far better to be dead with honor than to live with a name that has been stained by a lie. And so Jesus says the first category of sin is to defile a man, to steal from another man.

This passage of Scripture describes a second kind of stealing—that which a man steals from a woman. It too is just plain robbery. For one thing, Jesus says there is that which a man steals from a single woman. The words are sometimes used interchangeably, but most of the time *adultery* means an immoral sexual relationship between married persons, and *fornication* refers to an immoral sexual relationship between persons, one or both of whom are single. Why does God forbid fornication? Why does He say the vessel is to be possessed in honor? Why does He say not to be joined to a harlot? Because the Holy Spirit in you is involved in a physically defiling relationship—the sins of fornication, and adultery are unspeakably terrible things.

The young man who steals the purity, the virginity, the holiness and wholesomeness of a young woman, steals from her something that can

63

never again be replaced. She loses something that is unattainable again. I am not putting all the blame on the boy, for the fault often lies as much with one as with the other. Women love much deeper than men. It is much more possible for a man to experience a sexual relationship out of love and marriage than it is for a woman. When a woman gives herself to a man in a sexual relationship, she is giving much more than her body. She gives her heart, her soul, her ego, her will, and her self. She gives everything, and nothing can ever replace it. The man who takes a young woman's virginity robs her of the possibility of being able to face God, her husband, and the children that she has borne in honor and integrity and say, "I am completely yours." She carries something to the grave from which she will never, ever be the same. Fornication scars the personality of a young woman far worse than a young man. Boys say to girls, "If you love me, you would." I say, if you really love her, you wouldn't because love seeketh not its own. If you love that girl, if you honor and adore her, you won't steal that which is unspeakably precious to her well-being—her purity.

In this same passage Jesus also speaks of that which a man steals from a married woman. Adultery, as well as fornication, comes from the heart, and it too defiles a man. God wants to protect you, and you can't come out of an adulterous situation without being hurt. The playboy philosophy is wrong; sex for sex' sake is not where it's at! The sexual act must exist within the boundary, confines, and context of a person's emotional and psychological faculties, which is impossible outside of marriage. When it does not exist in this context, it is neither fulfilling nor beautiful. It is a relationship in which people only get hurt, and God says, "I love you and don't want you to get hurt." Outside of marriage, sex hurts and defiles.

Jesus adds that evil thoughts can also steal from a woman that which is not a man's to take. Think about the thought power of the mind. The mind is able to create, to play and replay, and to reproduce and recreate past experience. The mind is a precious and powerful thing. Jesus said to guard your mind. In some lands today people are hung for rape. Rape is a sexual relationship with a woman against her will. The adulterer in his evil thoughts who demeans, who possesses, who destroys, who takes a woman in his mind, not only against her will, but without her knowledge, is twice the offender. Virtuous women would be horrified to know how evil men picture them. She is pure and virtuous; yet a man may rape her of her tender modesty because he has taken liberties with her against her will and even without her knowledge. A man who steals from a woman against her will and against her knowledge does an awful thing. Evil thoughts destroy and defile us.

Jesus reduces all the issues of life which defile the heart to that which a man steals from another man, that which a man steals from a woman, and third, that which a man steals from God—blasphemy. The word *blaspheme* means to insult something sacred. It is used in the New Testament as being synonomous with the unpardonable. The Holy Spirit is in the world for one purpose: to create in men the desire and the ability to serve God. To blaspheme God is to insult Him. Balsphemy disallows God from being God in our lives and steals from God the right to balance and bless our relationship. Our religion is both vertical and horizontal. "Thou shalt love the Lord thy God with all thy heart; and thy neighbor as thyself." If you steal from God the right to be the controller of your life, you only steal from yourself.

Marriage is honorable in all things and the bed undefiled, made holy and beautiful because of the fulfillment which is the ultimate union of two personalities melted into the physical, emotional, and psychological wholeness for which they were created. That which defiles is anything other, or anything less; it is so because it makes of us less than the men and women that we can be in the totality of the perfect marital relationship with the right one and by His power. When He is allowed to be our God, He grants us the power to love. Then the forbidden fruit is not stolen, for it is hardly tempting. Many years ago a very wise man expressed it beautifully:

> Drink waters out of thine own cistern,
>   and running waters out of thine own well.
> Let thy fountains be dispersed abroad,
>   and rivers of waters in the streets.
> Let them be only thine own,
>   and not strangers' with thee.
> Let thy fountain be blessed:
>   and rejoice with the wife of thy youth.

THE FORBIDDEN FRUIT

Let her be as the loving hind and
    pleasant roe;
let her breasts satisfy thee at all times;
    and be thou ravished always with her love.
And why wilt thou, my son, be ravished with
    a strange woman,
    and embrace the bosom of a stranger?
For the ways of man are before the eyes of
    the Lord,
    and he pondereth all his goings.

(Prov. 5:15–21)

10

The Perfect Bond

Husbands, love your wives, even as Christ also loved the church, and gave Himself for it; That He might sanctify and cleanse it with the washing of water by the word, That He might present it to Himself a glorious church, not having spot, or wrinkle, or any such thing; but that it should be holy and without blemish. So ought men to love their wives as their own bodies. He that loveth his wife loveth himself. For no man ever yet hated his own flesh; but nourisheth and cherisheth it, even as the Lord the church: For we are members of His body, of His flesh, and of His bones. For this cause shall a man leave his father and mother, and shall be joined unto his wife, and they two shall be one flesh. This is a great mystery: but I speak concerning Christ and the church. Nevertheless let every one of you in particular so love his wife even as himself; and the wife see that she reverence her husband.

Ephesians 5:25–33

Many persons today play games with marriage by modifying it to make it compatible with the age in which we live. But when marriage is no longer compatible with an age, the age needs changing, not marriage. In any case, several variations on the marriage theme are being tried as possible substitutes for the monogamous, "till death do us part" kind of fidelity that used to be the ideal.

Communal marriage. Of course, the idea of communal marriage is a contradiction in terms. These unnatural relationships are neither marriage nor very communal, and they can only result in the gradual dehumanization of the people involved.

Trial marriage. It is starting to look as if that's what most marriages are these days. Vows are taken, but with mental reservations. Husband and wife are suspicious of each other and assume that unless things go well, they will forget the whole thing. Such marriages just don't measure up to what marriage can be.

Play marriage. Play marriage occurs when people live together and act as if they are married even though they haven't taken any vows. They enjoy long conversations together. If they are students, they discuss their professors and their courses. They have sex together; they may even quarrel a little, just enough to make it interesting. But they haven't laid their lives on the line for each other, and anyone who knows what marriage really is cannot help but feel sorry for them. You cannot play at marriage.

Great problems arise in the personalities of those who get involved in deficient forms of marriage such as these. While they think they are smart in their pursuit of variations on the marriage theme, they outsmart themselves and pay the penalty.

We need the Bible's help when it comes to the

subject of marriage. And it might surprise you to know that the biblical view of marriage is not prudish, narrow, or sexless. It's practical, and it grows out of God's real understanding of who we are. It is a view of marriage that is based on self-less love and creates a situation in which a man and woman so unite as to be one—completely one!

I suppose that ordinarily we think about the Bible as a stuffy, excessively spiritual book which represents a bothersome point of view designed to take all the fun out of life. But when we read Ephesians 5, we find that is not the case. To be sure, Ephesians 5 says that men should love their wives, and that idea, perhaps, contradicts some of the sentiment that is around these days. But did you notice that men are told to do this, not simply because it is a very considerate thing to do, or even because it will make God very happy, but because it will benefit them greatly.

"He who loves his wife loves himself." This is really the key to the Bible's description of the conduct that is appropriate for married people and of the great beneficial effects such proper conduct can have for people who express it. Ephesians 5 does not suggest that loving one's wife is an altruistic act, that is, an act of self-sacrifice on behalf of someone else, for that person's benefit alone. The Bible gives the impression that the man who loves his wife is going to benefit just as much as she will.

Isn't the Bible telling us that the union between a man and a woman that can exist in marriage is, ideally, a good deal more intimate, and even radical, than we think it could be? The Ephesians passage makes reference to the fact that already in the opening verses of the Bible, it is said "that a man shall leave his father and his mother and be joined to his wife and the two shall become one." When we first hear that we tend to think of the "oneness" exclusively in physical terms. We know that unfaithfulness does violence to this physical union and is consequently abhorrent from a biblical point of view. But the Bible's recognition that when people are married they become one is much more than that. No longer are individuals independent entities. Their very personalities are modified so that in a sense henceforth each must describe himself in terms of the other. The husband is not a personality by himself, but he is a personality in relationship to his wife. And the wife is not a personality by herself, but she is a personality in relationship to her husband.

How else can you explain the fact that the Bible says, "He who loves his wife loves himself"? Now it is true that the Bible takes the physical very seriously in describing the way a husband and a wife complement each other. It says that husbands should love their wives as their own bodies. But even though the body is the link that holds a husband and wife together, the Bible will not allow us to describe their relationship exclusively in physical terms. The Bible says that men are related to their wives as Christ is related to the church, and this is a very sublime and significant relationship.

There is something hard to take about all this. Today great emphasis is placed upon the importance and development of the individual personality. Thus, when the Bible talks about two people being so close to each other they can be called one, we tend to shake our heads and put the Book down. But maybe the reason is that our view of personality and personhood is actually very deficient. Maybe the Bible isn't wrong, but we are. Look where our emphasis upon the independence of each person has got us. In the realm of sex, for example, it has sent us scampering down the road of sensate satisfaction. We are willing to consider just about any sexual activity legitimate so long as people enjoy themselves. And maybe the Bible's description of the fulfillment of human personality within the framework of marriage is something we must look at very carefully.

When Ephesians 5 discusses the way a man and a woman become one in the context of marriage, it reflects the teaching of Genesis 1. "So God created man in His own image, in the image of God created He him; male and female created He them" (Gen. 1:27). Humanity's sexual characteristics enable men to reflect the image of God. God created man (that's "man" in the sense of "mankind") male and female. This is a very complex matter, for according to the Bible, marriage is directly related to the very being of man. Those who despise marriage and make it a plaything do themselves a great deal of damage and do damage to all of society. Marriage is exceedingly important, and when, in the providence of God a man is given a wife, he must take that fact of his life seriously.

The Bible says a man must love his wife. If you are wondering what that means, reread and ponder Ephesians 5. In addition to reaching out to her, talking with her, thinking with her about their mutual problems, and developing common interests and concerns, from the beginning of the marriage the husband is to consider himself one with her, with all that implies. So the Bible says, he who loves his wife loves himself. Marriage is that intimate, that mysterious, that marvelous. It involves the very modification of the personalities of the people who enter this holy state. If that principle could be recovered, there would be hope again. And if you recover it in your life, there will be renewal in your marriage.

11

Ride Those Wild Horses

In his book, *Ride the Wild Horses,* the late Wallace
Hamilton has done us a great service in pointing
out that man is a mixture of countless drives, impulses, and instincts. They are natural and God-
given, not of our own manufacture. And most of
life boils down to a struggle to resolve the question
of what to do with what we are. The need for
fulfillment of the sex drive is far more than a
biological craving. It is a need for responsibility,
for security, for a total blending of the fulfillment
of the being of which sex is only the expression.

Deep inside man the drive rages, and reasoning,
going astray, often goes something like this: What
I am is natural. What is natural, therefore, is good.
What is good is of God. Therefore, fulfillment in
life is to be found in a philosophy which suggests
that those wild horses within me, those drives and
impulses of which I am comprised, be allowed to
run loose. "Let her rip, brother, let her rip," is the
freedom cry of the new morality, but it is hardly
new at all. It is as old as life itself. The history of
the world is the history of man defying his passions, worshiping those powers within himself,

which, being greater than himself, are beyond himself. In Diana he defied sex. In Baccus, his appetite. In Jupiter, his drive to fight, to control, to possess, to conquer, and to kill. This philosophy of self-assertion implies no control of the sex drive or any other drive.

There is another philosophy which is as equally unakin to the ethic of the New Testament as is the philosophy of self-assertion. It is the philosophy of self-denial.

The Buddhists teach a state of Nirvana in which a man denies what he is and attempts to destroy his passions, to denude his personality, and to reduce all passion to nothing. According to this philosophy, the most spiritual among us are those boiled heads of cabbage who sit on the front row of church with no make-up, no class, no style, no color, and grunt like so many pious pigs. If the one philosophy would take the bridles off all passion and let the horses run loose, the other would take all of the fight out of them and beat them to death. It is possible to follow this second philosophy so far that a man can burn himself alive in the streets of Vietnam and so stoicize himself that he actually feels nothing.

But the sex drive as a focal expression of the totality of all being, which flows into oneness in the blending of the marriage relationship, fits perfectly, as do all of the drives of human personality, into neither camp. Jesus spoke of man as ideally being meek. The Greek word for meek which Jesus used carries the idea of wild horses running loose and then being bridled so that they can be controlled. The horse still runs as far and as fast.

He is just as powerful as ever, but he is under control. He is using his power purposefully and with direction. Remember that sex must not be understood in terms of mere physical gratification, but in terms of an expression of the entire personality finding its psychological blending and fulfillment in the person of husband or wife. Sexual intercourse in marriage, therefore, is God's point of contact between an unfulfilled person and His provision for fulfillment. As with all emotions and drives, sex is holy and noble. In that respect we agree with the proponents of the self-assertion philosophy. But their premise leads them invariably to the wrong conclusion, and sex for sex' sake is their erroneous answer.

This is my answer and I think it is God's: *Being made in the image of God, all of our power, drives, and impulses are God-given, God-honored, and Godly. Therefore, there are no sinful emotions. There are only sinful uses of the emotions.*

Repeatedly in the Scripture, different Greek words are translated as sin. The best, I think, and certainly the most commonly used is "missing the mark." A sinful act comes up short; it misses the point. It short changes life's capabilities and devalues the dollar of life. It is a counterfeit, a gip. Sex with the wrong partner is a sin which misses the mark. You will recall that adultery is not simply wrong because God forbids it, though that would be sufficient. But God forbids it because it hurts people. It gips them and fails to produce all that sex as an expression of total union with God's ideal counterpart intends to be. It promises much but does not deliver. It offers what it cannot produce, and both parties are shortchanged. God does not forbid adultery because He does not want you to have any fun but because He wants the best for you. Sex with anyone other than God's intended right one is not the best. It disappoints and it hurts, and God does not want us disappointed and hurt. He wants us happy and fulfilled.

The unmarried or the divorced, widowed, or never married can ride those wild horses, too. Call it sublimation or what you will, but you can control the sex drive by restraint, by shifting this drive of life into other areas until such time as marital fulfillment is a possibility. Then the unspent sexual capacity can create a virility, a recirculating life-giving force and power in your life which can drive you to success and send you to the top in life. Apart from the wonderful union of ourselves to Him through conversion, the greatest gift He has given us is the union of two persons in wedded bliss.

Ride patiently, carefully, seeking His guidance to find that one person you need. Wait for that person and be sure he or she is the one. It is worth the wait; so ride those wild horses as you do!

12

Is Divorce Ever Right?

This chapter is not intended for the person who has been divorced or for the divorced person who has been remarried. Some of the most well-adjusted, beautifully related, and effective people I know are persons who have had a difficult marriage, divorced, and remarried, and made a wonderful go of it. I must say that they are loved and wanted and welcomed in our church. Our congregation and staff make an effort to provide a special opportunity for divorced persons. In our single adult ministries they feel they are a vital part of the fellowship of this church.

Jesus makes it very clear that there are circumstances under which divorce is allowed, and I think it follows that remarriage under those same conditions is possible. If you are divorced and remarried, but not under those conditions, should you divorce and patch up the old marriage? Absolutely not! Two wrongs don't make a right.

All through His ministry, Jesus was never as concerned with what happened in the past as with what was going to happen in the future. I marry divorced people after counsel under some circumstances. I am far more concerned that two individuals have profited from a mistake and have objectively and honestly faced the problem of what went wrong and have taken steps not to bring the same ingredients of an earlier failure into a new marriage. What two people intend to do now is far more important than making a theological football of what went wrong in the past.

If I understand anything about the Christian gospel, it is that it is conciliatory by nature. It means new beginnings, a second chance. It is good news for tough situations. *When confronted with a woman who had had seven husbands, Jesus never once raised the issue of seven divorces but spoke of the woman's repentance and sincerity with regard to the future.* I never find Jesus condemnatory except to the self-satisfied who judge others. I always find Him more concerned with picking up the fragments of a difficult situation and helping people to start over. "Here is another opportunity," He says. "Do better next time and profit from the past."

Jesus makes it very clear, in my opinion, that there is a condition under which divorce and remarriage are permitted. The condition is adultery. There are a lot of shades of difficulty in that. There are a lot of problems which constitute an adulterous relationship. What about homosexuality? You could go so far as to consider the case of a man who is so proud and impossible that he is married to himself or to his job or to his business. If you want to make a theological football out of it, the truth is that it is possible to take either side of the case and argue the point. If you want to argue it, then argue it. But after all is said and done, Jesus never tried to reduce the gospel to a set of doctrines and precepts within a framework of dos and don'ts. He came and stamped across a thousand laws and rules one word—LOVE. The entire tenor of the conciliatory nature of the gospel causes me to say that two people who have profited from a mistake and are genuine in their love for the Lord have a beautiful chance to start again.

But I am concerned in these pages with those who may one day contemplate divorce. Jesus taught that marriage was never intended to harden people. It should be the most softening, intimate, and beautiful of life's earthly relationships. Seldom, however, is it given time to jell, to mature. In Reno you must be a resident six months to buy a hunting license, but you only have to live there six weeks to get a divorce. Consider these problems of the divorced.

1. *Loneliness.* The divorcé looks forward to his freedom, but too often it is freedom to be alone.

2. *Frustration.* This does not stem simply from the guilt that is induced by a puritanical society. Questions about one's own self-worth abound. Deep wounds remain in the heart of one who has lived through a divorce.

3. *Remarriage.* Statistics show that the second marriage has a much higher risk of failure than did the first. Only the Christian has any real hope. Once the trend is set, miraculous help is required in order to break the cycle.

4. *Envy.* What about his new wife? Or her new husband? And what about the days with the kids

and the relatives and the curious neighbors?

5. *Alimony* and *child support*. The young divorcée finds it is not nearly as easy as she thought. A judge told me recently that if a man really wants to get out of it, you can't make one out of one hundred pay his alimony. He says for every one the police have tracked down, there are one hundred they don't have time even to begin to look for. Think a long time before you consider divorce.

Notice that when asked about divorce, Jesus didn't even answer the question. (Mark 10:2–12). He spoke about how beautiful and binding marriage is. The questioners had to force the issue; they had to rephrase the question a second time before He would discuss it. Then He said that divorce is never directed. It was never intended. It is only tolerated. It is never what God would have prescribed. It is always only second best. It would be far better to have followed His guidance and found His right partner in the first place.

Jesus told His disciples that they were the salt of the earth and that if their right hand offended them, they should cut it off. Did He mean that they were literally salt and that if they sinned with their right hand, they were literally to cut it off? I think not. One, then, must raise the question, "Did Jesus mean what He said or did He mean what He meant?" One must interpret His teaching on divorce and remarriage in this context. The entire thrust of the Christian message is Good News! Good news about a second chance. Pick up and go on from here. Do better next time. Go and sin no more.

Recently a lovely young woman twenty-four

81

years old came into my office. She married at seventeen, became pregnant at eighteen, and divorced at nineteen. Her husband had abandoned her. I do not know whether there was sexual unfaithfulness involved or not, but there was certainly unfaithfulness to her sexuality as a woman. He was unfaithful to all of her needs, to the totality of herself as a person. She was abandoned and alone for five years, forsaken by a husband who has now chosen to become nonexistent. She had become acquainted with and chose to love a fine Christian man who loved her very much in return. He promised security, respect, fulfillment, a home, and a future for herself and a father for her child. What should I tell her? Can she marry him or is she to be relegated to a prison house of her own suffering for fifty or sixty years, shackled to the mistake of a former marriage to a worthless man? Hardly! I found myself asking, "What would Jesus say?" And I thought of the woman at the well and the woman caught in adultery and of a million like them who have been bound up, blessed, and forgiven and sent off again with His blessed, "Go thy way and sin no more." Three months later I joined the woman and her new husband in marriage.

Everything about the teaching of Jesus indicates the sanctity, the holiness, the permanency of marriage. Divorce, He said, is permitted because of the hardness of our hearts, but from the beginning it was not so. We are dealing here with how to save marriage, not destroy it. But the hard fact is that some marriages are already broken, already dissolved. What have we to say to those who long for a second chance to try for marital happiness? To them I say, "Go and sin no more. Go, and God go with you. Go, and God bless you." But, if you go, be honest with yourself. Don't blame the other party for your previous failure. The second is more risky than the first and the third than the second. Seek professional help. Get good counseling. Objectively analyze your first marriage. Lay it all on the table. Talk about it. What went wrong? What factors contributed to its break-up, and what is different now? Then make double sure, triple sure, that this time you did find that one perfect blending, meshing partner for whom God originally intended you, for marriage must never be a trial and error matter. The second marriage need not be second best. But a vastly more serious effort is required to find the one who was Mr. Right or Mrs. Right all the time, for only then can remarriage be right.

13

Love in the Bedroom

The creation of man was an act of genius. God said of every other creation, "It was good." But of man, "It was *very* good." Made in God's own image, the touch of the Divine was in his soul, the light of heaven upon his face. So bright was the glory that covered him that he and his bride were naked but knew it not.

In his original state of perfection, man knew absolute completeness and perfect fulfillment, but God looked ahead to the day when man would make a fatal moral choice that would cost him his contentment. God created a God-shaped vacuum in man that nothing else could fill, a point of potential contact with the Divine, a place where he meets his Creator, a place in which only God can dwell.

Thus, in completing the perfect simile between God and His own, between Christ and His bride, and that of a man and his bride, it became necessary that the intimate union of man and wife be just as physically, just as literally, a possibility. The act of divine justification, the return again of estranged man to intimate and perfect union with the one from which he was taken and of which he was once a part, has its perfect corollary in the conjugal state. As Christ's bride came from deep inside His own being, Christ having given His very soul for her life, so the woman, given life from within man when he gave of his rib, the nearest place to his heart, finds her deepest fulfillment in return to him in the sexual union.

Within the soul of husband and wife there cries the deepest of drives, the drive to express the fulfillment that is the completion of two beings, made for each other and fulfilled only by each other through intercourse. The sexual apparatus of both partners is the consummate zenith and physiological composite of all the nerves, membranes, tissues, cells, and emotions of the entire physiopsychological totality of being. In the genius that is the divine wonder of the sex act, it is only fitting that the blending of soul and being into the fulfillment of oneness for which two incomplete people have been perfectly prepared occurs deep inside the body. A body which is the physical conductor of psychological and spiritual being thereby becomes the agency to receive the physical tool that is the apex and the vehicle of the giving of one's very self and soul.

Paul speaks of a man being "in Christ" and adds that we are all baptized at conversion by His Spirit into the oneness of perfect union with His body. We are actually born into His being. Just so, the physical union that is sexual intercourse between two persons becomes the thrust and force of two beings striving for the perfect union of body and soul.

Jesus said the greatest commandment is to love the Lord with all your heart, mind, and soul. But these three are harbored within a physical body. When the willing bride (the believer) opens her being, heart, mind, and soul, to the heavenly Groom, He comes to live with her. And where does He live? Within the body. Thus, Paul could say Christ is "in you," the Hope of Glory. Likewise, the physical union of marriage becomes the vehicle of the total union of being and occurs within the female body.

Jesus said if a man be joined to a prostitute, he is one with her. He is joined not only physically but in being. And then he asked, "Don't you know that your body is the temple of the Holy Spirit," and that in essence in adultery we join the Holy Spirit in an immoral and adulterous union? As a man apart from God cries for Him from which he came, so in the sex drive a man and his bride cry for each other from which they came at creation. God did not have to make it this way, but He chose to. He could have made Eve as He did Adam, without the help of another human being. But He chose to take her out of her bridegroom's body as He did His bride from His body, that she too would crave again the oneness that once was theirs. Sex, then, becomes the sacred expression of oneness that is marriage.

Let every couple, therefore, honor sex by learning to call all sexual terms by their proper medical names. Unfortunately every sexual expression has a proper name and a "dirty" counterpart. The serious-minded adult should delete the latter from his vocabulary. Sex, as the consummate expression of being into oneness, is the highest and holiest gift of God from one human being to another. Forget what you have heard or read in gutter language. We are talking about a sacred experience, something holy, something divine.

While sex, as the language of love, may in a sense be a language without words, at no time is the verbal expression of affection as appropriate as before, during, and following sexual intercourse. During the sex act, the being of man and wife are striving as fully as possible for total union, being that is lodged within the physical body and centralized in the sexual organs, now united. The rib, as the nearest place to the heart, was the original point of mutual physical union. But God has created the union to occur, not from the side, but from the front of human bodies. Why? The reason is obvious. We humans are lovingly and divinely created by Him to be the only creatures on earth that may experience sexual intercourse while looking into each other's face. With our eyes, the gateway to the soul, we may speak without talking, while with our lips we may speak as well. Well did the psalmist say, "We are fearfully and wonderfully made."

When a married couple loves, they should speak of their love. They should speak with their bodies, their eyes, their voices, their touches, their caresses. And they should speak tenderly, lovingly, and slowly, words beautiful and proper. The married pair should never refrain from speaking anything and everything they feel. If any movement or position is particularly displeasing or particularly pleasing, it should be expressed.

87

Early in marriage the husband will have to pause to wait for the orgasm of his wife, restraining his own. As the years come and go, she may well need to learn to wait for him. As the young couple learn the unspoken language of sex, the language of the touch and the caress, the verbal language may become less and less necessary, but words are always appropriate.

We have seen that sex for sex' sake, sex without the commitment, responsibility, and security of marriage, is a gip. But sex in marriage can also be this kind of sex. Two-minute sex may reduce a relationship to two-minute love. Commitment that is true fulfillment, union that is forever, cannot be cultivated exclusively on the basis of physical gratification. Love, real love, is far more than feeling. It is knowing, and knowing involves time. When she was informed she was to have a child born of heaven, the Virgin Mary aptly responded, "How can this be, seeing I *know* not a man." The expression "to know" has long been used as the heavenly language of marital union. Love is time and time is talk, that is, face to face, the language of the eyes and the language of the lips.

The thoughtful and loving husband will proceed patiently, slowly with his bride, knowing that his greatest pleasure is her fulfillment, not just that his ego is fed because he has "satisfied his woman," but because he is the one man who is the fulfillment of her being. The husband is the man without whom she is not a whole person, either psychologically or spiritually. She is what she is because of him, and he is what he is because of her. That is what Jesus meant when He said,

"The twain shall be one flesh," completely one.

I advise a young couple to wait a period of time, at least four or five years, before having children. Never again after the birth of the first child can the wedded couple ever be totally and primarily preoccupied with each other. Always the needs of the child will be first and those of the partner second. There is ample time for raising children. The early years should be kept exclusively for learning to know and love each other.

Often in marital counseling I am asked the question, "What is normal?" What is normal with my husband or wife in frequency of intercourse or place, position, length of time, or regarding oral or genital sex? What is normal is what is mutually pleasing to both of you. What is right is what is right for you. But a few words of caution. Sex for mere sexual gratification may diminish sex and destroy it. Trying something different simply for the sake of variety may be offensive to one partner. It should not be planned; it should be natural, automatic, as mutually acceptable as it is naturally progressive. When intercourse is so regimented that it comes down to, "Well, it's Thursday night again, Charlie," it is in danger of losing the emotional naturalness that makes it an expression of true feeling. Sometimes spontaneity should take precedence over the precaution of regimentation. Or, as Ann Landers says, "The older you get the more you may have to jump on the train while it's passing through!"

Conversely, sex stimulated only under unusual circumstances is indicative of a sick marriage and one in need of professional help. When you seek counseling on the sexual or other aspects of your marriage, select a person in whom you have professional confidence. He or she may be a professional marriage counselor, a doctor, a psychologist, a psychiatrist, or a minister, but he or she must not be one of the guys at the office or one of the girls in the bridge club. When you need help, get professional help, and get the best!

We have seen earlier that there is a vast difference between "being in love" and "loving." While "being in love" is not enough to sustain a marriage, certainly the more emotional and romantic involvement the better, particularly in the bedroom.

What first attracts two people to each other? What is the electricity that occurs across a crowded room between two people who have never even met before? It is a physical attraction, and it is normal and good. But the courtship tends to magnify the pluses while marriage amplifies the minuses. The only pluses we see at first are all physical, and it is those which are the most obvious, as well as the most easily relaxed. Whatever else you do, major on keeping sharp those physical qualities which first made you attractive to your spouse.

Jack Jones sings a popular song in which he exhorts wives always to be lovers too. One of the lines says: "Don't send him off with your hair up in curlers. You may never see him again. Day after day there are girls at the office, and men will always be men." Good advice, Mr. Jones, and let me add, don't invite him to bed with your hair up in curlers and cold cream on your face and expect him to get turned on. And, husbands, don't expect your wives to be responsive if you need a shave and maybe a shower. Keep yourselves physically attractive. Don't get fat. Don't let down. Work at it. It can make or break a marriage!

We have seen that intercourse between husband and wife is the patient, verbal, physical, intimate blending of two personalities ideally suited for each other and created to find complete fulfillment within each other. It is the internal union within the body of the woman of the hearts, minds, souls, and wills of two beings, with the body serving as the vehicle of that union. Earlier we have reminded ourselves that from the base of the brain, the totality of emotion, nerve, and being flows down the spinal column to the base of the spine, across the bottom of the trunk of the body, and culminates in the penis of the man and the clitoris at the top of the vagina in the woman. During the union of the male and female sex organs there occurs the blending of being. Sex, therefore, cannot survive of itself, but only as it is a union of plus and minus—a consummate harmony between need and fulfillment in one's perfect opposite. In her orgasm, or climax of sexual intercourse, the wife is sensitized to a total release of self with a flood tide of surrender and release in harmony with her husband. The twain have become one flesh. Likewise the husband's orgasm brings a physical climactic release of living sperm that is the giving of his very life to her. Their lives are one, as are their bodies. A perfect union has occurred between two persons who are incomplete of themselves and whole only as they are each completely, a living part of the other.

14

Love All Around

As we have seen, there are several major problems of adjustment in marriage: personality differences, falling out of love, sex, and so on. Let us explore briefly several other problematic possibilities.

1. PROBLEMS WITH RELATIVES

Jesus makes it very clear that entailed in the new one-flesh union is the forsaking of prior commitment to mother and father. But it is not a leaving which entails complete and permanent separation. A healthy relationship with one's in-laws is greatly to be desired in the well-adjusted marriage.

The question, "Who gives this woman in marriage to this man?" and the customary response, "Her mother and I," should ideally be precisely that—a cessation of the parents' claim upon the daughter and a commitment of her future well-being to her husband. But the psychological break is not quite as easily achieved as are the spoken words at the ceremony. Basically there are two problem areas in this realm: (a) the continued possessiveness of the parents, and (b) overdependency of either member of the young couple on either parent.

Well-meaning parents are apt to mettle and advise when advice has not been solicited. As a general rule, parents should create an atmosphere of healthy interest which says to the new couple, "We are here, you may fall back on us. You may depend upon us, but we are not here to initiate assistance. You may not feel our presence, but you will know that we are available if you need us and ask for our help." An occasional call or visit, when announced in advance, is always appropriate, but those visits should be less frequent than are the visits from the couple to their parents. Contact between the two parties should be originated mostly from the couple and be perhaps twice as frequent as are the visits from the parents. This will give the couple a sense of security in knowing that their parents are there and that they are interested without feeling overpowered by their presence.

Let me add very clearly, under no conditions except those of absolute dire emergency should a couple live with either set of parents. No house is big enough to be a home for two families. The influence of the parents upon the adjustment of a newly wed couple is difficult enough at best without the dominating presence of well-meaning parents under the same roof. While there may be emergency exceptions for a short duration, no couple is financially prepared to be married who must plan at the beginning to move in with their parents. The young couple's dependency upon their parents can be equally dangerous. It is not normal for a young man to take his wife to spend every week-end with his parents, and to go hunting with his brothers and eat his mother's home-cooking. At the most, once a month is probably too much.

Assistance during dire emergencies may be acceptable, but only with absolutely no strings attached and no speeches from the father to do better next time. The father who has not prepared his son in fiscal responsibility before he marries has waited too long to start. In short, relatives should be loved and respected, but generally at a distance after marriage, with most of the contact being initiated by the couple. A tendency to spend an excessive amount of time with parents on the part of either party can be a sign of immaturity and may require serious personal counseling.

2. COMMUNICATION

Fully 25 percent, if not half, of the couples with whom I speak are having problems that should have long since been resolved or never happened in the first place. Serious problems have arisen because they are feeling the same thing, but are simply not saying it. Their inability to communicate verbally has amplified their problem into a mountainous catastrophe. It is amazing how little things are catapulted into major devisive problems simply because two persons will not talk. We human beings are the only creatures with the gift of intelligible, verbal communication, and yet we talk the least and fight the most! Most major problems are the outgrowth of something very small. The couple who cannot communicate about sex or in-laws today is the couple who could not communicate about picking up dirty socks in the bathroom yesterday!

Sexual relations are a time for verbal expressions of affection, but verbal expressions of the heart and mind should be made at absolutely every level of married life from socks to sex. One must be able to receive the opinion of one who feels differently on a given subject without taking it as a personal attack. The difference makes the difference. Unless you can learn to communicate verbally with tolerance and compromise on little things, the big things may well drive you apart.

Marriage is a fifty-fifty proposition. That "Mr. Plus" is not necessarily a plus because he is the stronger, more domineering of the two; he is not a plus because he is *better* than his wife but because he is *different* from his wife. At least 90 percent of the time the two should be able to communicate to the ultimate point of agreement. Only rarely will the differences be so irresolvable that the husband as head of the home will have to make a decision in contrast to his wife's opinion. Most of the time when I have come to that point and made a decision independently from my wife, I have regretted it. Husbands, a good wife, a godly woman, is a heritage of the Lord. Listen to her. You don't always have to be "Mr. Right."

The popularity of the late-night talk shows is only a slight indication of the hunger within the heart of human beings to express themselves verbally, to know as they are known. Body language is beautiful and very easily read. A man can say very much with his eyes and body to a woman and she can to him. But while some things cannot be spoken, there are some things that only words can say. Ultimately, there is no substitute for the verbalization of feelings. You simply must learn to talk. In our society we have a built-in life-style which makes it difficult to communicate. Perhaps 90 percent of the leisure and recreational time of all Americans is spent in entertainment by a third party or third medium. Television, movies, comedians, sporting events, all involve a husband and wife seated side by side with little communication with the third party and none with each other. Yet this is the way most Americans spend their time. How can we know each other? How can those pluses and minuses begin to fit? How can marriage become what it is psychologically and spiritually intended to be if two people give little or no time merging and meshing their separate selves?

Tonight, just for a change, I urge you to try something. Turn off the television no later than 9:00. Go into another room and sit with your wife on a couch with a soft light and talk. Talk? Yes, just talk. It will probably take you an hour to start talking, really talking. But if you are to become one, you must know each other; and if you are to know each other, you must talk.

3. MONEY

One of the most consistently difficult areas of marital conflict lies in the area of money. Let me suggest briefly six or seven practical, but eminently important, helps in this difficult area.

Keep money in its proper perspective. The Bible does not condemn money. To the contrary! It states very clearly that "it is God that giveth thee power to get wealth." It is the insatiable desire for money that God deplores. God does not say, "The rich will fall into a snare," rather, "they that *would be* rich." In other words, those who want to be rich for riches' sake. Jesus clearly said, "You cannot serve God and mammon." Rather, "Seek ye first the Kingdom of God, and His righteousness; and all these things shall be added unto you." That is His formula, His way; make a God of God, put Him first, and the rest of life will begin to fall into place.

Immediately after marriage, better still before, the husband should take out a sizeable insurance policy with his wife as the beneficiary. She may be young and beautiful and could easily marry again, but she also may become pregnant on her wedding night or become disfigured in an accident on her honeymoon. Don't wait. No excuses. No exceptions. Get an insurance policy, a good one, preferably before you get married.

Coupled with your financial relationship to God, the decision should be settled before the marriage ceremony as to your responsibility to the

Lord and your responsibility to others. Ideally you should pay the Lord His tithe first and secondly save 10 percent for yourselves. And then after adequate insurance, you may live as well as you can on the remaining 80 percent of your income. A well-balanced family economy is centered in doing what you can for yourself while asking the Lord to do what only He can for you. Tithing invites God into your affairs and makes Him your financial partner. Through the years I have found that the couple that will give God 10 percent, save 10 percent, and live on the other 80 percent will have few financial problems.

Watch credit buying. Ten dollars down and ten dollars a month can cave in on you when multiplied too many times. You don't have to keep up with the Joneses. You don't have to impress anyone. A three-hundred-dollar car can get you down the road just as well as a three-thousand-dollar car if you are in a financial tight, and the only thing that will be affected will be your ego. Far more important than that is your own peace of mind relative to your financial well-being.

Bill consolidation can be a sound financial decision if made in consultation with a good banker. Immediately establish a personal relationship with a banker. Visit him early in your marriage, well before you need to make a loan. Let him know you and your financial position. Seek and follow his wise counsel in fiancial matters. Set up a joint checking account and joint savings account with all personal financial matters in the name of both parties. You are one flesh, one personality, and everything humanly possible should be done to enhance the thrust toward unity in your lives. From time to time it may be necessary in business matters for the husband's name to appear exclusively on legal documents; but a will (which should be made before marriage), insurance policies, property, charge accounts, and bank accounts all should clearly define the wife as the partner and beneficiary.

It might surprise you to know that I have dealt with at least three divorces which arose exclusively over the matter of separate checking and/or savings accounts. In my opinion, it is bad psychology to do anything which separates the two. One home, one life-style, one name, one bank account, one interest, one religion—everything should be done to enhance complete merging of the two into one.

4. RELIGION

I have said much in preceding chapters about the husband/wife relationship as symbolic of Christ's relationship with His bride, the body of believers known as the church. Marriage is a spiritual relationship. It merges a hundred thousand personality parts into one complete entity, and it is a divine transaction which can only be perfectly accomplished by the miraculous presence of the Spirit of God which oils the meshing, moving parts. Two persons must know and love Christ and be possessed by His Spirit. Further there must be a unity of the total religious relationship.

Husband and wife should be of the same denomination. They should belong to the same church and go to it regularly. If one is a Presbyterian and one a Catholic, a period of time should be set aside with an equal number of instructional sessions with the minister of each church. After a set number of sessions, sessions which have been approached by intelligent, mature, open-minded adults, if an agreement cannot be made, then a compromise on a third church should be reached. I would strongly advise a member of my congregation to join the denomination of his or her husband or wife rather than be permanently divided in church affiliation. Regular attendance together in one church gives a horizontal as well as vertical relationship to the entire Christian experience and is an inseparable part of the life of the seriously minded married.

But religion at church is not enough. A daily time for joint Bible reading and prayer can be one of the most important ingredients in a marriage. It is here that we really know each other, as we talk to each other and talk together to our heavenly Father. Hearts are laid bare and insight into personality given as we lay ourselves open to Him in prayer. Let them scoff if they will, but it is still vitally true: "The family that prays together, stays together."

Certainly every individual is freely responsible to God for himself, and the time may come when children will wish to chose a denomination or even a religion different from that of their parents. But in the early formative years of life, children should have been pointed in the direction of the church of their parents, assuming serious responsibility for their religious education, remembering always the admonition of Scripture, "Train up a child in the way he should go, and when he is old, he will not depart from it." Note that the proverbial writer said, "When he is old," not, "When he is young." Regardless of the very best in religious education, sometimes even the best of children, during their teen-age years, will depart from the faith of their fathers. But the promise is that the seed will ultimately bear fruit. Perhaps not as quickly as we would like, but it *will* produce that fruit, and when they are old, they will return to the Lord.

The very first book of the Bible tells us that God was pleased with His creation of man, but that it was not good for him to be alone. God ordained that man should have a wife to love him and to be loved by him that they might, "Know and complete and fulfill each other." Solomon said, "He that getteth a wife, getteth a good thing." And Jesus said, "For this cause shall a man leave his mother and father and cleave to his wife and the twain shall be one flesh." A miracle? A gift of heaven? A psychological experience? An experiment in living? Yes. It is all of these and it is more! It is and can be a taste of heaven on earth when God is allowed to teach us and mold us into what we can never be without Him and without our spouse, a fulfilled person, a complete personality.